VENERABLE ARCHDEACON
CAVANAGH OF KNOCK

FIRST IMPRESSION, JUNE 1953
SECOND IMPRESSION, DECEMBER 1955
THIRD IMPRESSION, APRIL 1967
FOURTH IMPRESSION, JANUARY 1972
FIFTH IMPRESSION, APRIL 1976
SIXTH IMPRESSION, MAY 1978
SEVENTH IMPRESSION, DECEMBER 1978
EIGHTH IMPRESSION, DECEMBER 1983
NINTH IMPRESSION, JANUARY 1984
TENTH IMPRESSION, MAY 1988
ELEVENTH IMPRESSION, MAY 1989
TWELFTH IMPRESSION, MAY 1990
THIRTEENTH IMPRESSION, JULY 1991
FOURTEENTH IMPRESSION, JULY 1992
FIFTEENTH IMPRESSION, APRIL 1993
SIXTEENTH IMPRESSION, AUGUST 1994
SEVENTEENTH IMPRESSION, JUNE 1996
EIGHTEENTH IMPRESSION,
NEW EDITION, MARCH 1997.
FIRST IMPRESSION, AUGUST 1997

PRINTED BY ROSCOMMON HERALD, BOYLE

Venerable Archdeacon Cavanagh

Pastor of Knock
(1867 - 1897)

Liam Úa Cadhain

Published by

KNOCK SHRINE SOCIETY

Nihil Obstat :

JOSEPH CUNNANE, S.T.L.,

Censor Deputatus

Imprimatur :

✠ JOSEPHUS,

Archiepiscopus Taumensis

Die XVI MENSE MARTIS MCMLIII.

DO CUM GLÓIRE DÉ AGUS
ONÓRA NA hEIREANN

———————

This little publication is dedicated
to
the Ever Immaculate Mother of God

Foreword to the New Edition

THIS year, 1997, marks the Centenary of the death of Archdeacon Cavanagh, and will be commemorated at Knock Shrine with fitting ceremonies on September 7th. It is over forty years since this short biography was put together, and since then, it has run to eighteen reprintings. In the light of Ireland's present prosperity, the accounts of the Famine and the years of agrarian unrest, may now appear to be almost beyond belief, nevertheless, that was our history. In 1953, when the book was written, the memory of recurring famines in the West, right up to the time of the Apparition, was still almost a reality to people well aware of the suffering endured by the generation or so before their own. Archdeacon Cavanagh had lived in the midst of the famines and experienced their after-effects during the whole of his priestly life. Was it perhaps providential that a man who was well known for his compassion was at Knock then to give hope to his afflicted people. Many believed at the time that it was because of his great spirituality that Knock was singled out for that unique Apparition. In the first edition of the "Knock Shrine Annual", we carried an article on

Archdeacon Cavanagh, and over the past fifty-eight years, some aspect of his extraordinary life was brought regularly to the notice of readers. It could hardly have been otherwise; from the outset, he appeared to have been a major figure in the history of the Shrine, even though he had not himself witnessed the Apparition.

Looking over this short account of his life, it is clear that Archdeacon Cavanagh was noted for his exceptional devotion to the "Ever Immaculate Mother of God" from his early college days right until the end. His compassion for the suffering souls in Purgatory was also outstanding. Many foreign journalists and other commentators came to Knock in those early days, and were received by the Archdeacon in the modest thatched cottage where he lived for almost thirty years. The foundations of that cottage are now being marked and preserved. Those journalists told specifically of the long hours he spent in the confessional, and today, a very large number of the thousands of pilgrims who come to the Shrine, seek the special blessing of reconciliation. Is it perhaps possible to see the pattern of that faithful commitment to the confessional evolving yet again? Because of steadily growing numbers, the first chapel of reconciliation, built in the sixties, had to be replaced with a much larger one in 1990, a remarkable development in these perplexing times.

Equally remarkable is the continued and ever increasing devotion to the Holy Souls. A special Mass is celebrated for them every Friday at the Shrine and hundreds more are offered on their behalf each year at the request of the Shrine Handmaids and Stewards and many other generous donors.

Another very important development at the Shrine was the building of the Blessed Sacrament Chapel in 1983 where perpetual adoration is now part of every day's devotion. How clearly all of these developments focus again and again on the extraordinary holiness of the Archdeacon, of whom it was said by the "Weekly News" in 1880, "of the time he can call his own, the greater part is spent before the altar of that church now linked with what may be perpetual fame."

Fame for that church is now a reality, and its inspiring Shrine representing the Apparition in every detail, where so many Masses are offered and countless rosaries recited is a haven of peace and Divine mercy. There, Our Lady of Knock who came to us as the crowned Queen of Heaven, continues to lead all souls to repentance and a deeper love of the Eucharistic Lamb of God.

As we greet the centenary of Archdeacon Cavanagh's death, let us return thanks to God for the man who in his life was revered for his "extraordinary sanctity", "his boundless charity and self-denial", his love for the Blessed Sacrament, his labours in the confessional, his compassion for the souls in Purgatory, and his abiding devotion to the "Ever Immaculate Mother of God". How pleased he would be to see all of these devotions which were so dear to his heart flourishing at Knock Shrine today. May he continue to petition Our Lady of Knock to grant all our requests for soul and body, and help us to make Knock Shrine more widely known as a special "House of Prayer to all Nations".

Siobhan C. Bean Ua Cadhain,
Bridgemount.
19th March, 1997.

Preface

*I*T is a pleasure to commend this brief Life
of Archdeacon Cavanagh written by District
Justice Coyne. In rescuing his memory from
oblivion for the benefit of the present
generation the author is not only paying a
well-deserved tribute to a great priest and a
devoted client of the Immaculate Mother of
God, but is adding to the many services he
has already rendered to the Shrine of Our
Lady of Knock. As a small boy I had the
privilege of seeing Archdeacon Cavanagh, a
venerable and imposing figure, during one of
his visits to my native town. I remember how
greatly he was revered for his sanctity, for his
life-long devotion to our Blessed Lady, and
for his unwavering faith in the Apparition at
Knock. With great skill the author sketches
the background of his life. He was ordained
the year before the Famine of '47 took its
terrible toll from our people. As Curate in
Westport during that tragic time Father
Cavanagh showed the abounding charity
which was one of his marked characteristics.
Untiring in his labours he made heroic efforts
to bring relief to his stricken flock. Later as
Parish Priest of Knock and Aghamore he
exhibited all the qualities of the true pastor

of souls, ministering faithfully to the spiritual needs of his people, and in particular spending long hours in the Confessional for the benefit both of his parishioners and of strangers who sought his advice. His life was simple, austere, and self-sacrificing. Though his resources were limited, he was always generous to the poor. Through all his years as a priest he never ceased to preach devotion to Mary Immaculate and to inculcate fidelity to her Rosary. He must surely rejoice to see how Knock has developed into a great centre of pilgrimage where our Blessed Lady is honoured by the vast number of faithful clients who annually visit her Shrine. may this Life make the saintly pastor of Knock better known, and help, as he would wish, to keep undimmed the true pilgrim spirit of prayer and penance in all who come to the Shrine that was so dear to his heart.

✠ *JOHN CARDINAL D'ALTON*

ARA COELI, ARMAGH
May 27th, 1953.

Venerable Archdeacon Cavanagh

14

Archdeacon Cavanagh outside his little thatched residence where he lived for close on 30 years and for which he had a deep attachment because of the many favours he had received there through Our Blessed Lady.

The Church at Knock in 1879 showing Apparition Gable.

16

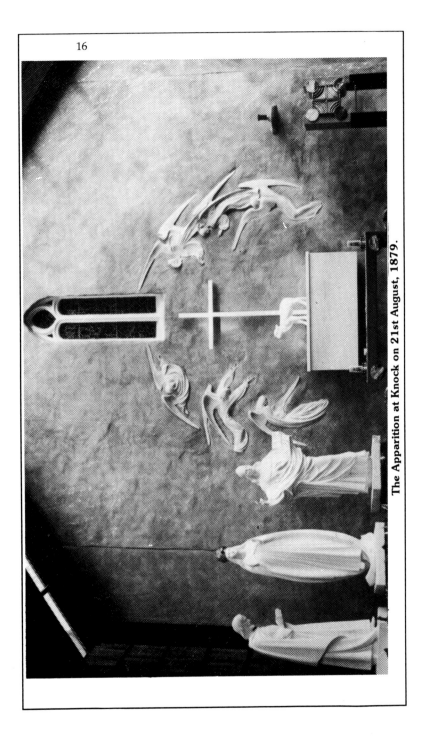

The Apparition at Knock on 21st August, 1879.

CONTENTS

We wish to express our gratitude to the Librarian, County Sligo (Miss Niland), for the use of the files and extracts for the illustrations at pp 55 to 59 and also 61; to Mrs. McDermott of Derrykinlough, N.S., for her kind assistance in taking the extracts at p. 60; and to the Librarian, National Library, Dublin, for the use of extracts at p. 54.

The prints at Sligo and Derrykinlough, N.S., belong to the series presented by Mr. Hunt of Philadelphia, U.S.A., where he discovered old newsprints of "The Graphic" (London) for the period 1879-1880.

Prologue

TO write of Archdeacon Cavanagh as Pastor of Knock Parish at the time of the reported Apparition there, in 1879, appears to begin at the end of the story

It was not easy to decide on a suitable inscription for this little book. There are so many equally relevant names at hand : "The Priest of the Apparition"; "The Pastor of the Irish Shrine"; "The Priest of the Famine"; "A Priest of the Land War." However, the title selected was the one generally associated in the minds of the people with Father Cavanagh of Knock.

The fact that we entitle this book "Venerable Archdeacon" suggests at once, perhaps, that preference is given to the period when he was a very senior priest and advanced in years, but the account will touch on every phase of his life from childhood to death in outline.

It may be well to state here that the use of the prefix "Venerable" in this connection is the ordinary courtesy title applied to the dignity of an Archdeacon. It has nothing to do with the proceeding in which the word is used in the early process of an official investigation by the Congregation of the Sacred Office.

In fact, it was only in 1875 at the age of fifty-four that the honour of Archdeacon was conferred on him by the great Archbishop John McHale of Tuam, who never placed his honours lightly, nor did he suffer fools gladly.

For over twenty years prior to his appointment to Knock, Father Cavanagh was curate of Westport (1846-1867) and there he had many anxious days during "Black '47" famines.

As the full story of the life and times of Archdeacon Cavanagh is unfolded there will be no difficulty in overcoming any fixed unfavourable prejudices that may have been formed about the subject of this short account, and we feel that in a spirit of fair play the reader will accept the duly authenticated evidence left by clerical and lay contemporaries (some of them still living) of this kindly, simple and intensely spiritual priest.

The Archdeacon was a man whose priestly life was of a very quiet, unassuming, solid nature. His was a sort of piety that was the envy of his critical colleagues, and a puzzle to his friends. To some he was merely a "pious fool"; or, no less crudely, "a pious humbug"; to others just a subject for table pleasantries.

Whatever the view of the envious and the puzzled, there is no doubt at all that the Archdeacon was a man who followed severe penitential exercises, down even to the hair-shirt; was deeply devoted to his holy office, to his people and to the souls in purgatory, and he had an ever consuming desire to promote Our Lady's Cause, for whom his favourite title was "The ever Immaculate Mother of God."

In writing the Life Story of anyone, there is always the biographer's dilemma as to whether, or not, it is more impressive to write very near the time of the subject, or, at a distance of years. In one you have the heavy, often biased, criticism of colleagues; in the other, there is the factor of uncertainty due to the passage of time.

Now that Archdeacon Cavanagh is dead for more than half a century it will occur to some that it is time to collect and record verified facts bearing on the life of a priest who was so devoted to Our Lady and who had the remarkable distinction of filling the office of pastor at a time the parish was favoured by a reported vision of the Blessed Virgin.

As we shall see in a later chapter Archdeacon Cavanagh lived at a time of periodic national revolts, preceded and followed by counter measures of repression at the hands of an alien, unsympathetic government whose cult was coercion and more coercion.

In the vital five years, 1845-1850, we had a coercion Act passed each year as the only contribution by the English Government, for relief in Ireland's hour of sore distress.

At the same time it would be ungrateful to

overlook acknowledgement to the people of England who organised in 1847 The British Association for Relief of Distress in Ireland.

One of the members, who was also a news correspondent, travelled to Ireland seeking first hand information and the following is a record of what he found :

"I have been for the past few weeks resident in Letterbrick, Capital of the barony of Arderry, Co. Kildare.

"The Barony contains 180,000 acres of land, over which is scattered a population of 30,000 souls. The union work-house is 31 miles distant; besides that, there is neither hospital, nor dispensary of which the poor can avail themselves at the present moment.

"Two-thirds of this vast extent of land is divided between two proprietors — Mr. Black and The Mulligan.

"The Mulligan is chairman of a relief committee, which he never attends. He has given no money, or food, whilst he has extracted all he can from the soil. He pays no taxes, builds no cottages or farm buildings, supports no schools or hospitals. He and his family own about 40,000 acres of land.

"At Killala where the gentry clamoured loudly for seed (at half cost) the sailing boat, **Lightning,** was sent with 350 sacks, of which she sold one . . .

"There is at this moment fever in half the

houses in Arderry — I call them houses by courtesy, for they are but hollow, damp and filthy dung-heaps.

"The people sell their last rag for food, and are then forced to remain in their hovels until the weakest sink from hunger. Their festering corpses, which they have no means of removing, then breed a fever which carries off the rest.

"On my arrival here I found the soup-kitchen on which the lives of hundreds depend, stopped, not for want of funds, but because the vicar and his curate, having £130 intrusted to them jointly by our association, had quarrelled, and preferred seeing the parishioners starve to making soup for them."*

Irish history of the period 1821-1897 tells us of unrelieved hardships resulting from recurring artificial famines — there were four in the time of Archdeacon Cavanagh.

The days of open persecution, priest-hanging and banishment had just passed and at the time of the birth of Bartholomew Cavanagh we were within eight years of partial emancipation, after which priests were no longer outlaws and Catholic laymen were first admitted to the various professions — doctors, lawyers, dentists, surgeons.

During his whole priestly life (1846-1897) Fr. Cavanagh's experiences brought him through

* Mr. J. Higgins — Letter to the Times, 22nd April, 1847.

some of the most trying periods of Irish history. The decades were marked by a series of hardship and hunger; evictions and emigrations; risings and reprisals. But in all of these, Archdeacon Cavanagh had that great virtue of charity which characterised his whole life, as well as a rare gift of spiritual direction, which was devoted entirely to everything that meant the safety of the souls entrusted to his care.

CHAPTER I

Birth — Education — Ordination

THE Cavanagh family was a rather unusual one. They had lived at Annaghdown, Co. Galway, since the days of the Cromwell invasions. The place is, perhaps, better known to many as **Anach Cuain,** in which Raftery, the Irish poet commemorated the drowning tragedy that took place between Annaghdown and Galway, where nineteen people were lost in September, 1828.

The ruins of a great pile on the south-eastern shore of Lough Corrib showing, even in its advanced decay the old beauties of Irish architecture, mark the site of a one-time famous Abbey of Canons Regular. Nearby stand the crumbling walls of an equally famed nunnery, of whom St. Brigid (sister of St. Brendan) was a distinguished member.

Not only had the place such distinction but it was also a diocesan centre, the diocese of Annaghdown — having its own Cathedral, a fact now long forgotten.*

It appears that the Cavanaghs were an old Catholic family who were substantial landowners in County Carlow at the time the drive "to hell or to Connaught" was enforced by

*Walton's History of Ireland.

the invaders and they paid the price of dispossession for their faith.

John Cavanagh and his wife, who had been Kate Browne, had thirteen children, five boys and eight girls. Bartholomew was born in 1821 and was baptised in Corrandulla Church, Co. Galway, by Fr. Keogh. The boys, evidently, were favoured by a good education. In addition to Bartholomew becoming a priest, there was another boy, John, the eldest son, who was ordained for the Tuam Archdiocese also, and ministered as Parish Priest of Killerein 1849-1872. One of the boys, Thomas Robert, qualified as a veterinary surgeon when the law permitted Catholics to enter the various professions after the Emancipation Act of 1829. He appears to have been a prominent and successful surgeon, as he held a commission for buying re-mounts for the British Army and for that purpose attended all the big horse fairs in Ireland.

Two other brothers — Patrick and Willie — lived in the old home for some time.

In the famine of 1846, fifty acres of potatoes belonging to the family rotted in the ground, and, like many others, the Cavanaghs were ruined in consequence.

The two boys emigrated to America and in a short time built up a thriving business in New York City, where both of them died, long before the Archdeacon.

Bartholomew showed a taste for study and every sign of a vocation for the priesthood. His parents were in the fortunate position that they were able to send him to school in Galway where he attended every day, making the long journey on horseback.

On his attaining a suitable age Bartholomew was sent to Tuam Diocesan Seminary, where he completed his preliminary studies in preparation for Maynooth College.

As a student he was called Aloysius, his second forename, taken at Confirmation. His full name, Bartholomew Aloysius, was very fitting — Bartholomew after the Apostle and Aloysius after the Confessor. The Apostle was remarkable for his zeal, while the Confessor was outstanding in his innocence.

The boys in the College preferred to call him Aloysius as they saw so much in common between the young student and his second patron.

During his whole College course young Cavanagh continued to distinguish himself by his piety and innocence. Whilst in Maynooth, and after, he was known to practice special devotion to the Mother of God. From the very dawn of reason this devoted child of Mary loved her and served her.

FIRST APPOINTMENT WESTPORT

Bartholomew Cavanagh was ordained in 1846, and his first appointment was to Westport as Catholic Curate.

"The town of Westport was itself, at the time, a strange and fearful sight, like what we read of in beleaguered cities. Its streets crowded with gaunt wanderers, sauntering to and fro with hopeless air and hunger-struck look, a mob of starved, almost naked women around the poorhouse clamouring for soup tickets. Our Inn, the headquarters of the road-engineer and pay-clerks, was beset by a crowd of beggars for work.

"The survivors were like walking skeletons - the men gaunt and haggard, stamped with the livid mark of hunger, the children crying with pain, the women in some cabins too weak to stand. When there before, I had seen cows at almost every cabin and there were, besides, many sheep and pigs owned in the village. But now the sheep were all gone, all the cows, all the poultry killed — only one pig left. The very dogs which barked at me before, had disappeared — no potatoes, no oats."*

By one of those awful calamities with which Providence sometimes visits states, and nations, five millions of people forming an integral portion of a flourishing and mighty empire, are entirely deprived of food, and consigned to the horrors of famine. The Prime Minister is naturally and rightfully appealed to, to relieve the suffering part with an equitable application of the wealth of the entire body, and he replies to them,

* Reports. W. E. Forster.

to look to themselves, and rely on their own resources.

Self reliance is a fine theme when there is sufficient for any crisis; but to tell a people to supply themselves with food, when both food and means of procuring it are gone, appears like the requisition of the Hebrews to make bricks without materials.

Such is now the frightful state of this country, brought on, as it were, by a systematic collusion between the Irish landlords and the English legislature and to which Ireland never would have been reduced, had she the protection of a native parliament*.

In those terrible times the then active curate had frequently to anoint as many as forty dying parishioners before breakfast.

The Sisters of Mercy, Westport, devoted all their services and means in relieving the distress caused by hunger and plague.

They were on constant visitation to the houses in the district. Breakfasts were supplied to about 500 children every day (and sometimes up to 650) in the schools.

When the potatoes, the ordinary food of the poor, were destroyed by the blight the people flocked into the towns to avoid the fearful alternative of starving in the country.

* Archbishop McHale, Dec., 1846.

Previous to this awful visitation when isolated cases of distress occurred the sufferers were relieved by their charitable neighbours. But now all were in almost equal destitution and the poor people, as their last resource, crowded into those towns in which charitable institutions had been established for the relief of the poor and suffering. Were it not for the kind charity of the people of England, France, America and other places the Sisters could not have provided relief. The Holy Father, Pius IX, in the midst of his own trials of persecution and plunder, out of his solicitude for faithful Ireland, sent the very generous contribution of £100 for Galway and Mayo.

From America consignments of flour and meal, and about the same time large quantities of clothing came from friends of the poor sufferers in exile.

In the pockets of some of the articles were found a roll of biscuits or some confectionery carefully tied and inscribed "for a poor Irish boy," or, on a slip of paper pinned to the article, "my best coat for a poor Irish boy."

There is a record also of much charitable relief received from a Polish nobleman, Count Stereliski, who had contributed generously for the relief of our people. Even the Turkish Government contributed generous help for the suffering people of Ireland.

And by way of supplementing these sources of help for the needy, Father Matthew the great apostle of Temperance took occasion, in the course of his crusade tours, to deliver charity sermons wherever it appeared likely to produce results, for the purpose of providing contributions towards the relief of the famine stricken.

To meet the need of rendering assistance, five auxiliary "workhouses" were opened in Westport and large stores at the Quay, at Saltpans and in Altamount Street in the town.

These places were overcrowded and fever and dysentry broke out in several stores. Many of the Sisters of Mercy were struck down with fever. These Sisters were occupied amongst the starving and dying people and such was the state of ignorance that much time was spent in teaching them the mysteries of our Holy Faith in preparation for the Sacraments. The Convent funds were running out and provisions were advancing in price with the result that meat could not be bought and for breakfast and supper cocoa was used, as tea was too expensive.

The Convent records for 1867 have noted as follows:

"Our kind friend and holy guide the Rev. B. A. Cavanagh was appointed to the parish of Knock. This devoted priest was so good to the poor; so full of charity for all. He had not only nothing of the world's wealth but was greatly in debt.

"He was senior curate in this parish since 1848 and ordinary confessor to the Community for the long period of seventeen years. From this holy priest we had always experienced the most uniform kindness and the most zealous co-operation in every work of mercy undertaken by us."

Fr. Cavanagh ministered in Westport for twenty-one years. In the course of that time he was occupied with the arduous task of coping with the harrowing effects of the famine years.

Recurring hardships and a great lack of religious instruction combined to bring about the most lamentable moral lapses.

One of the most pressing needs was provision for the occupation of young girls. He therefore turned his attention to the task. While a suitable building was being erected the funds ran our and the work stopped. One day, it is related, when he was on the Lecanvey road near Croagh Patrick a stranger spoke to him about the new building and enquired the reason for the interruption. Having been told by the young priest there was no money the strange man handed him the exact amount necessary to complete it. The donor's name was never ascertained but the work was finished. It was piously believed that the mysterious donor was none other than St. Joseph. It was during the same trying period he sold his horse and watch to relieve the famine-stricken. To this day Fr. Cavanagh's name is held in the highest regard in the parish of Oughawall, where he was looked on as a saintly sagart of the poor.

CHAPTER II

Parish Priest of Knock-Aghamore

THE Rev. Bartholomew Cavanagh was appointed Parish Priest of Knock-Aghamore and transferred there from Westport in 1867. It was a decade when we appeared to be recovering from the effects of the famines of 1847 and the fifties and, generally speaking, our people were looking forward to a period of peace and plenty.

However, about this time, unfortunately, the Fenians split into Fenian and anti-Fenian Nationalists and unhappy differences developed between the Church and sections of the Fenians.

The branch of the Fenian-Nationalists argued that the Church had no right to interfere in what they called "their politics," and denounced the clergy as deadly foes of Irish Nationality.

The Priests replied that the leaders of that section of the Fenians had no respect for clerical authority.

It was most unfortunate that extreme elements whose doctrine was force alone became so identified with all national, open movements that we were unfairly represented by our enemies, even in Rome, with the result that our most popular movement was condemned.

Events in England, too, were disturbing. In this very year, 1867, the hanging of Allen, Larkin and O'Brien in Manchester, and the Clerkenwell prison explosion had not helped us at home.

All these disturbances kept the Nation in a state of constant turmoil and, unfortunately, when we reached the Seventies there was a still further calamity to come, as we shall see presently.

Such was the position the new Parish Priest of Knock had to grapple with. Happily, the pastor was about the age of forty-six, a time of life when problems have no great fears and difficulties can be taken in one's stride.

PROSELYTISM IN ACTION

One of the greatest sources of worry to spiritual shepherds at this time was the activity of the proselytiser. He was abroad everywhere. He was in the school; in the street; in the workhouse, busily engaged in trafficking in the souls of hungry, toiling peasants and the soup-school was his one last hope.

It is necessary to remember that only a few years previous to 1795 it was felony to hold any kind of Catholic School, or teach Catholic children, or give instruction to anybody. Hedge schools supplied the only way to gather the children for education. These schools were sheds during winter and rainy weather, and in fine weather the children were collected in the open.

When the Penal Laws were relaxed, but not repealed, the schools provided were rude cabins with turf seats along whitewashed walls.

The late Dr. McHale, Archbishop of Tuam, took a leading part with his priests, in opposing proselytism, in season and out of season, in all its hideous forms.

It was a well-known fact that the object of those who planned the system of so-called National Education in those days was the eradication of the Catholic faith from the country. But the inherent love of the people of Ireland for the religion of their fathers, the vigilance of their pastors, and, above all, the merciful care of an all-wise Providence, rendered the scheme abortive, and caused it to lead to results the very reverse of those it was intended to produce.

Within the Archdiocese of Tuam Dr. McHale established seventeen Convents of Franciscan Brothers to conduct Primary Schools for the education of Catholic children.

In one of his reports to Rome he referred to the so-called National Schools, known as Whiteley Schools.

There was, he said, no lack of schools in his diocese as there were Christian Brothers,

Franciscan Brothers, Sisters of Mercy and Presentation Sisters and therefore no need for the Whiteley Schools.

FIRST IMPRESSIONS

Father Cavanagh was fully aware, on his coming to Knock, that he had taken over the responsibility of a parish that had suffered much in the distress of the famine and he knew that the district could ill afford any margin beyond the need to exist. The barony of Costello had been rated at the lowest figure in the West of Ireland because of the inferior quality of the land.

On arrival at his new parish, and as one would expect, Fr. Cavanagh surveyed the place, the church, the residence, and the general state of the parish.

Let us first get an outline of the priest himself, and here is a word picture from the "Weekly News" :

"I must try in a few words to give an idea of the Archdeacon's countenance and manner. His forehead is lofty, his face long and full of healthy colour, his features regular and firm, his eyes blue, full and expressive, his whole air denoting gentleness and benevolence. He speaks with an easy fluency; his manner in conversing upon interesting themes becomes thoroughly energetic, and he occasionally used gestures with very telling effect to add to the expressiveness of his language. What charmed me most of all in him was his fatherly tenderness in speaking of his own people."

As will be seen later, every word of this pleasing portrait is borne out by Archbishop Lynch, Toronto (Canada), who had come on a visit of thanksgiving to Our Lady of Knock.

Now as to the Church. It was erected at the time Emancipation was passed. It was a stone building, cruciform in design and on the West outside wall there was a very remarkable — one would say prophetic — inscription :

"Matt. 11 chap. My House shall be called the House of prayer to all Nations.

Ps 117. This is the gate of the Lord; the just shall enter it.

Erected by the Rev. P. O'Grady, P.P., 1828."

The interior was poor of aspect. Beyond the unpretending altar, and two or three small windows filled with stained glass, there were no attempts at decoration, and very ineffective ones at convenience, since all the benches in the place would not seat more than thirty people. The floor was roughly flagged.

To say that the parish priest of Knock-Aghamore was self-sacrificing, devoted and unwordly is to state what all knew. His home was most simple, consisting of three rooms, all on the ground floor of a thatched cottage no larger than the habitation of the poorest. The bedroom, more properly called a cell, was scarcely large enough to contain a bed and small table. There was one living room which did duty for study and parlour. The kitchen opened on the street. His simple residence held an open door for mendicants, and the famine conditions brought many of them.

It was the moral state of the people that concerned him most. He knew that the hard times and the hunger of the famine had left a mark on the people in the small port-town community he had just left. But what of the rural parish ? They, too, had suffered the general neglect, the coarseness or looseness of manners that springs from disorder. However, there was no evidence that Sunday was forgotten and the Mass was respected and all unnecessary work avoided on the Lord's Day.

It can be easily imagined what was his first Sunday address to his new congregation. He told them of the dire conditions of the people he had left. How they were gathered into improvised workhouses in large numbers, dying of hunger and fever and how he had been called on to anoint as many as forty people of a morning before breakfast.

He asked the congregation to join him in thanking God that they had escaped much of the misery of the small town communities. He told them of the need there was to provide occupation, housing, food and clothing for the girls who were homeless and workless in Westport and whose abandoned state called for serious attention and for the need to teach them the elements of catechism. The evil due to drinking, too, was one of the causes of the great misfortunes amongst those people. He impressed on his hearers how grateful they ought to be that by the Grace of God they had no public houses in the whole parish of Knock, and twelve years after he was with great pride able to repeat the same claim in an interview with an English correspondent.*

One of the greatest sources of misery about this period was not the famine itself (and that was bad enough), but the effect of drink.

Our people, weakened by hunger, suffered more easily from alcoholism than the better fed.

The ravages of the evil were in evidence all round. It was the period when Father Matthew carried out his great temperance crusade. Father Matthew's efforts for temperance filled the city of Cork. Every street, every lane and alley, every large workshop had its story of marvellous change from misery and want to comfort and happiness. Every locality had its illustration. Everyone knew some wretched drunkard's home that had been converted, as if by the wand of a magician, into a scene of humble contentment and smiling plenty. And that was the same happy story wherever the Temperance crusade reached.

If it is true that the people of a parish very soon reflect the pastor then it is certain that the

---

* It is a remarkable fact that the first house licensed for the sale of drink at Knock was not obtained until 10 years after the reported Apparition.

people of Knock-Aghamore lived the full Catholic life under the influence of Archdeacon Cavanagh.

The only word of blame or disapproval expressed against the priest was that he was too devout to the Blessed Virgin; that he lived very much in contemplation; nor was he as practical as he might be in wordly matters of business, and perhaps, worst of all, he was a man who was never known to take a holiday.

IMPRESSIVE PREACHER

We have been assured that one of the remarkable facts about the Archdeacon was his great preaching ability when he addressed congregations on the subject of Our Lady. He was a man of mediocre talents as a student but his fluency of address on this subject held his people completely and was the surprise of his former class fellows.

A colleague's description of the Archdeacon when he addressed his people, either parishioners or pilgrims, gave one a very vivid picture of the pastor : At the usual time for addressing the congregation during Mass the Archdeacon removed his vestments and always proceeded to Our Lady's altar and there delivered a homily on the ever Immaculate Mother of God. The preacher entered so fervently into the subject of his discourse and imparted such devotion and animation into his address that the whole body of the congregation soon reflected the deep sincerity of the speaker. They always remained fully attentive and never seemed to grow tired however long the address.

We have, at least one instance of the Archdeacon's direct, simple treatment of the subject of his sermons. One gets from it a clear idea of his appealing manner of approach, obviously deeply touching by its simplicity of language and the sincerity of the speaker. The occasion was the Feast of Epiphany in 1882 :

"Let them remember that thousands and thousands and thousands are burning in hell fire, and thank God that they yet lived to escape it, if they pleased." And then he told them how they might escape that place of torment, and how they might secure for themselves the happiness of being the friends of God. He dwelt especially on the necessity of making their morning devotions well.

"Let each one of you," he said, "never neglect the sign of the cross the moment you awake from sleep. Remember that there stands at your bedside, watching you, the demon who wants to drag you down to hell by tempting you to sin, the good angel who watches you to help you to heaven. You must choose for the day which you will follow. If you make the sign of the cross at once, you place yourselves on the side of God, you choose His standard, and the devil will flee from you. When rising, you must praise and adore God for His goodness in sparing you to see another day. Never, never leave the room where you have slept, no matter what the hurry of your business may be, without saying, at least, three or four Our Fathers and Hail Marys, in honour of the ever-Blessed Trinity, to place yourself under God's protection for the day. This will only take you a few moments. Then you must offer to God all your actions for the day, that they may belong to Him ! Oh ! what merit you will have for any action thus offered to Him ! It will not take you very long to say — 'I offer you all my thoughts, words and actions to the honour and glory of God, into the hands of the Blessed Virgin Mary, in union with the Adorable Heart of Jesus, and the sufferings of my Divine Lord, for the souls in purgatory.' All our actions are thus consecrated to God, and offered to His honour and glory, and we leave all our actions at the disposal of the Blessed Virgin Mary for those holy souls who, when released from purgatory, will never forget us. They will pray constantly for us at the throne of God.

"One soul released from Purgatory gives more glory to God than the entire universe."

OUR LADY AND THE SOULS IN PURGATORY

The Archdeacon had always a great devotion to the souls in Purgatory. "It would seem as if this devotion, and devotion to the Holy Mother of God were inseparable. She is the Mother of her children above all, of her suffering children, and she is the Refuge of Sinners on earth because her arms and her heart are always open to those who suffer. She is also for the same reason the helper of the souls in pain."

And Father Faber, too, that great lover of Our Lady, points out that devotion to our dearest Mother is equally comprehended in this devotion to the Holy Souls. "Whether we look at her as the Mother of Jesus, and so sharing the honours of His sacred Humanity; or as Mother of Mercy, and so specially worshiped by works of Mercy, or, lastly, whether we regard her, as in a particular sense, the Queen of Purgatory, and so having all manner of dear interests to be promoted in the welfare and deliverance of those suffering souls," and, he continues, "how can a Mother rest content while her children suffer on earth? Sin is one great source of suffering, hence she uses that plentitude of grace which God has given her to help the sinner to become a saint. But for her dear children who suffer in Purgatory she longs as only her maternal heart can long. They are safe. So far, they are no cause of anxiety to her. But what mother is satisfied even when she knows her own son has escaped from a terrible danger until she has clasped him in her arms. So it is with Holy Mary, the faultless Mother of God, the God-given Mother of men. Hence she loves and rewards most abundantly those who assist her to attain the company of her children in heaven. And so the extraordinary graces granted to those who assist and pray for the souls in Purgatory."

This whole subject has a close bearing on the story of the Apparition at Knock. Several months before the Apparition, Archdeacon Cavanagh found he could gratify his holy desire of saying one hundred Masses for the Souls in Purgatory whom our Blessed Mother most wished released. The great poverty of the people deprived him of the temporal help which other priests have from the celebration of the Holy Sacrifice for the intentions of the people. He made it known that he rejoiced to find he was free to follow his desire and to offer the adorable Sacrifice for these holy Souls in Purgatory. It was after the last of the hundred Masses was offered that the Apparition took place on 21st August, 1879.

The work of the parish at that time called for the greatest alertness a zealous priest could arouse.

Parochial duties had to go on; Masses had to be arranged; confessions heard; sick calls attended to; hungry families fed; mothers comforted; evicted parishioners housed, somehow.

The little church building needed attention, too. A belfry was erected in 1872; in 1874 the donated stained-glass window was fitted; in 1875 the little parish choir was augmented by a new harmonium. All these activities were big events in the life of a small parish.

These things were not done to satisfy any personal taste of the priest but because he believed that the beauty of the house of God helped people to increased devotion.

THE PARISH SCHOOLS

There was only one school in the half parish of Knock, and two in the Aghamore end. The buildings called schools, were better described as cabins, while six teachers comprised the whole staff in the parish.

There was no Government Aid in those days. The Pastor had to provide teachers to help him in overcoming the state of neglect and ignorance in which the youth was brought up.

The task ahead required determination and never failing trust in God and Father Cavanagh was blessed in large measure with both virtues.

Thirty years after, it was some consolation to the Pastor to see eleven schools and thirty-two National Teachers appointed to care for the youth of the parish.

CHAPTER III

Ireland's Darkest Hour

UNLESS we bear in mind the actual conditions under which the Irish people were forced to live in the nineteenth century we shall be quite unable to appreciate the immense perils and difficulties, internally and externally, that faced our priests and their flocks.

It is most important, therefore, in the first place, to find that comparative history tells us that many secret confederacies were formed all over Europe in the 18th and 19th centuries, and particularly in those parts known to be Catholic in religion. All of them directed attention to some National grievance, and unfortunately Ireland had many, but behind the scenes it was recognised that the main driving force was implacable hatred of the Catholic Church and its teaching.

Early in the century, somewhere about 1820, the Ribbon Society was formed in Ireland and, like its counterpart on the Continent, it devoted its campaign towards some particular oppression in each district.

In Ulster it professed to oppose Orangeism.

In Munster it operated against tithe-proctors. In Connaught it was used against rack-renting and evictions where both evils were especially active.

The origin and control of the organisation was then somewhat of a mystery and the clergy, consequently, found it necessary to advise their parishioners to exercise great caution in any approach made to them by the agents.

The Ribbonmen worked under many titles : "Liberty Men"; "Religious Liberty System"; "United Sons of Irish Freedom"; "Sons of the Shamrock."

There is no difficulty in recognising even in these phrases, the influence of the French Revolution of 1789 on all such organisations.

In the years preceding historic 1798, the Directories of the Illuminati, a body of Atheistic Freemasons, had its emissaries in Ireland and they were active amongst the ranks of the United Irishmen, like those who were sent amongst the Catholic Carbonari in Italy.

At that time, France was in the hands of Atheistic Masonry and for it own ends it sent us the expedition that arrived at Killala to found the Irish Republic, an Atheistic Republic, of course.

The whole undertaking ended in complete failure. The French abandoned and sacrificed our young men to the tender mercies of the English at Ballinamuck.

The only help that the Mason Body gave

Ireland, was to teach us how to conspire in secret, oathbound, and often murderous league against our oppressors.

"J.K.L." AND SECRET SOCIETIES

Ribbonmen, Molly Maguires, Fenians, were entrapped into those secret bodies and became ruled by unknown but world power Atheistic leaders.

The young Irish boys of the rank and file who entered those organisations were completely innocent of the power and purpose behind the various bodies.*

It appears there were some common, well-recognised approaches in the general plan for the spread of these secret bodies :

(a) Wherever there appeared to be any public grievance they seized the opportunity seeming to redress the claim. But it was only a pretence.

(b) To exploit and enlarge any difference of views arising between priests and people in any parish.

When it is remembered that the political upheaval in the life of the French Nation was part of the considered plan of World Freemasonry it will come as no surprise that Ribbonmen appeared in Ireland within a short

* "The Grand Orient Freemasonry Unmasked."

period after the blood bath of Paris.

The Ribbonmen Society, as far as can be ascertained, operated in Ireland in full vigour from 1820 to 1880.

In November, 1822, the Patriot Bishop Doyle of ·Kildare-Leighlin (better known as "J.K.L.") found it necessary to address his pastoral letter to the deluded and illegal association of Ribbonmen :

> "We address ourselves chiefly to you who may have been seduced into any illegal association, but above all, into this vile and wicked conspiracy which has been lately detected and exposed in Dublin and which is known to have extended into some parishes of this diocese.
>
> "But before we do so we take you to witness this day, that we are clear from the blood of you all; whereas for three years we have not ceased night and day, with tears admonishing everyone of you to desist from these illegal associations, which have always augmented the evils of our country, and now tend to bring disgrace upon our holy religion.
>
> "Whilst with you on our different visitations, we did not cease to forewarn you of those things. In our pastoral instructions, printed and distributed amongst you, we explained at length the nature and tendency of these associations - their folly - their injustice - their opposition to all the laws, human and divine, which

you were bound to obey.

"We explained for you the impiety of the oath which connected them together; and the clergy in their respective parishes have not ceased to labour with us in this sacred duty. Yet we will not address you in the language of reproach; we will not, above all, rebuke you, dearly beloved, for the obstinacy and perverseness of a few amongst you; but, as the object of our ministry, is not to destroy, but to save, not to call the just but sinners to repentance, we will once again admonish even those few, however perverse, hoping through the influence of the Holy Spirit that they will attend even now to our instructions, and be at length converted from their evil ways."

Towards the middle of the last century Ribbonism was on the wane and its methods had been gradually changing, softening its punishment from full scale murder, to mild threats or just mutilation. It will be observed that here, too, we have the true masonic pattern in operation. In its initial stages in any area, the full blast of terror in every form - murder, torture, banishment were freely inflicted, until the people showed by their reaction that they were definitely against such crimes. Then the lesser menu of punishment was introduced, to prevent the populace from revolting en masse.

As a matter of political and economic history it will be of assistance if we glance, cursorily, at the headlines of some of the leading events in Irish affairs from the beginning of 1800 to the end of the century :

1829 Catholic Relief Bill granting Emancipation (in part)

1830 Repeal of Act of Union launched by O'Connell.

1831 Tithe war rages against Tithe collectors; Ribbonmen Association spreads.

1844 O'Connell's Repeal meeting banned at Clontarf and the Liberator arrested.

1846 Famine decimates the land owing to failure of potato crop.

1847 Evictions for non-payment of rent; Emigrations.

1848 John Mitchel arrested and transported.

1850 Failure of potato crop.

1866 Fenian rising planned but anticipated and crushed.

1867 Manchester martyrs and Clerkenwell explosion.

1879 Land League formed by Michael Davitt; Bad harvest and Famine.

"On the 11th February, 1848, Mr. Labouchere referred in the House of Commons to the havoc in one year on board the Irish emigrant ships sailing to Canada and gave the following appalling figures :

" 'Out of 106,000 emigrants who during the last twelve months crossed the Atlantic for Canada and New Brunswick — 6,100 perished on the voyage; 4,100 on their arrival; 5,200 in the hospitals, and 1,900 in the towns to which they repaired. The total mortality was no less than 17 per cent of the total number emigrating to those places; the number of deaths being 17,000.'

"The country that has lost in thirty years one-third of its population — a million by famine and two million by despairing flight — must have received a well-nigh mortal wound.

"No glozing fallacies, no heartless theories have availed to stamp upon the Irish Famine and Exodus any character less dark than that of utter calamity. Yet Ireland has survived the blow."*

These facts will help us to realise how disturbed were the conditions in the country at the time.

We had the sorry spectacle of aggravation and provocation on the part of the government with all its ruthless repressions and incitement.

There was one obvious reason for all this. It was one of the plans to provoke a rising under disadvantageous terms.

In the midst of this disorder the secret societies were busy availing themselves of full opportunity to further their secret oath activities.

And finally, to fill the cup of sorrow to overflowing, our people suffered the calamity of a potato-crop failure in 1847, 1850, 1879.

* A. M. Sullivan, "New Ireland," p. 390.

There was one hope to sustain our people. We were just out of the penal period in which the Mass was proscribed throughout the land. "Ireland had learned how often the blood of the priest and people were mingled with the sacrificial Blood of the Victim; people and priest, and Mass book and Altar and Lamb going down together in one overwhelming holocaust."*

Then our forefathers crowded nearer to Mary. They were rosary-minded, always faithful to the family rosary, and in all their troubles turned to the Mother of Sorrows. And so it was now, too, when every thing seemed black as night they clutched their rosary beads ever tighter. With a confidence to which the Irish people were deeply loyal, they fled to Our Lady for that protection which she promises is never left unaided.

* Miss M. O'Connor, Knock Shrine Annual.

54

Sligo Courthouse (and police barracks) where Davitt, Killeen and Daly were charged with sedition following a meeting of the Land League in Gurteen, Co. Sligo, November 2nd, 1879. (Extracts from "Illustrated London News", 4th December, 1879.

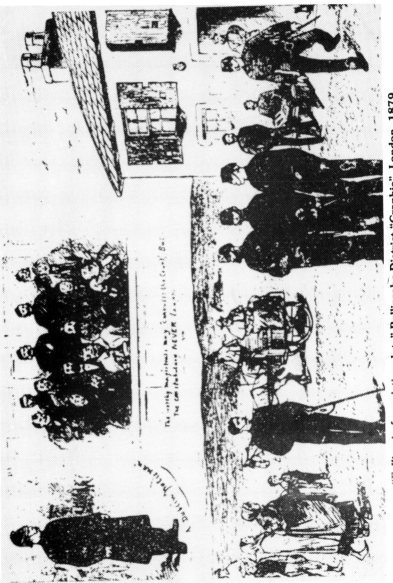

"Falling in for eviction duty" Ballinrobe District "Graphic", London, 1879.

The picture represents the group of Orangemen labourers and their 2,000 military escort brought from Ulster in 1879 to harvest Captain Boycott's crops during the Land War. They are seen at Ballinrobe on the way back to Ulster with Boycott's cattle, having given up the siege at Lough Mask. The amount of the crop saved was valued at £350, while the cost to the State was £3,500. It was one of the great victories for the "silence of ostracism". ———————"The Graphic", London, 1879.

"Widow and dying child". "The Graphic", London, 1879.

A roadside dwelling.   "The Graphic", London, 1879.

A poor man's cabin.   "The Graphic", London, 1879.

"A friendly visit : no work; no credit".

The Graphic", London, 1879.

After the eviction.

"The Graphic", London, 1879.

CHAPTER IV

The Year 1879

SECTION I — THE LAND WAR

THE year 1879 opened a new chapter in the affairs of the Irish people. It is marked by more than one very remarkable event. In the order of time these events may be cited in the following manner :

1. The Irish Land League was founded in Mayo by Michael Davitt.
2. The reported Apparition of 21st August, 1879, at Knock.
3. The Oath-bound Secret Society defied and broken in Mayo.
4. The potato crop failure of 1879 was the last of the famines.

The rents of 1877 were paid mainly on borrowed money. The losses on one crop alone — potatoes — was, this year, £5,500,000, making in two years, on this crop a loss of about thirteen millions sterling.

The harvest of the year 1878 was a failure though an advance, in some respects, upon that of the previous year. Moody uneasiness intensified. Every small farmer in the country had been heavily borrowing of late on the strength of prosperous 1876.

The harvest of 1879 was disastrous. On the potato crop alone there was a loss of £7,200,000 in that year. No rent was earned, yet the rent was paid in full. It was very like the desperate efforts of 1846 and greater energy than ever was put forth to retrieve the losses but with little success.

From the late Rev. Fr. Jarlath, O.Cist., Roscrea, preaching at Knock in 1937, we get the following picture:

"For Knock, as I knew it, in my boyhood days, 50 years ago or more, so unlike the world-famed Knock which it is your privilege to behold to-day, was but a little way-side village of some dozen houses more or less, among them the little church itself, a school-house and the parochial residence. And such a parochial residence . . . I remember it well — Archdeacon Cavanagh's house, a long, low thatched cottage. No wonder the portly Archdeacon walked with drooped shoulders, for he must have bent double to pass through the low-framed doorways of his parochial residence.

"Add to these a police barracks on the rise of the hill, a post office and a few little shops, and you have Knock of 1879. And the social condition of the people in and around Knock in those days was in every respect akin to the social condition of Nazareth in the days of Our Lord — poor, peaceful and unknown, dead to the outside world, rich only in the treasures of faith and grace, in their devotion to Christ and His Blessed Mother, the Way of the Cross and the Rosary, meet soil, surely, for the benign gaze of divine complacency and love.

"Oppressed like the rest of the West in those days with the curse of despotic landlordism and ever-recurring famine, the year 1879 was the worst, perhaps, on record since the desolating famine of 'Black '47'.

"How well I remember that historic year, 1879 — the potato blight and the ensuing famine, the Indian meal dole, otherwise called 'the committee meal', the relief ticket, the workhouse van.

"No wonder, then, was it that as of old God looked down with compassion on the distressful land of Juda and Israel He loved; so now too, He looked down with similar compassion and pity on the famine-stricken, faithful people of Holy Ireland. How like God's chosen people, the Israelites of old, were the good and faithful people of Ireland in those days. Going, they went forth, sowing the seeds of their faith in beads of sorrow."

The housing and living conditions were so primitive that the ravages of the dreadful disease, typhus fever, then raging, decimated the countryside. The poor tenants were prevented from making the smallest improvements to their dwellings. An extra window, or the changing of a window, the insertion of a kitchen chimney, or the least essential addition called for an increase of rent from the landlord. The result was that the houses, rightly called hovels, were certain breeding grounds for all sorts of disease.

The Communities of the Sisters of Mercy at Claremorris and Swinford, and the Sisters of Charity, Ballaghaderreen, found ample outlet for their great work of charity.

These Sisters dressed, washed and coffined destitute women and often carried the remains into the street. Were it not for their work of mercy the dead might have remained unburied, indefinitely. Several committees were formed to relieve the crying distress.

Amongst these were the Dublin Mansion House Committee and the Ladies' Land League, through whose exertions and assistance many thousands were saved from premature death.

One priest in the vicinity of Knock declared, "in the presence of God," that three hundred and fifty families in his parish would have died of starvation were it not for these voluntary relief committees.

That was the period when a group of patriot writers were attached to the **Nation,** amongst whom was the brilliant young lady contributor, "Speranza" (Lady Wilde).

They poured out verses of encouragement and hope for our sorely distressed people.

By Irishmen at home and abroad "Speranza" was hailed as a beacon of light in one of the darkest moments in Ireland's history. Her pungent, patriotic verses included — "The

Exodus," from which we make a brief quotation:

"A million a decade ! Calmly and cold
The units are read by our Statesmen sage :
Little they think of a nation old,
Fading away from history's page :
Outcast weeds by a desolate sea —
Fallen leaves of humanity.
. . . .
A million a decade ! what does it mean ?
A nation dying of inner decay —
A Churchyard silence where life has been —
The base of the pyramid crumbling away :
A drift of men gone over the sea,
A drift of the dead where men should be."

In the winter of 1878 the Irish farmers woke up to the terrible fact that, on the hazard of yet another crop, that of 1879, their very existence hung.

The desperate rack-rents of the rising times lay heavily on them. They were deeply in debt to the Banks, to the guano agents, and seedsmen. Yet, at all sacrifices, and at any price, further credit must be had, or means obtained to put in the 1879 crop and tide over the months to the Autumn of that year.*

The people were faced with a refusal of the British Parliament to do anything to help the country, to remedy the heavy grievances suffered under landlord rule, and now multiplied by the prospect of another famine.

* "New Ireland," by A. M. Sullivan.

Notices of eviction had increased five-fold, and a new wave of crime broke out in the South and West.

It was on the 28th of April, 1879, that the Land League first took shape at Irishtown, Co. Mayo, under Michael Davitt's leadership.

The objectives of the League were to combine all the small farmers' grievances. No more evictions, campaigns, or landlord shootings. No more agitations, or debates, or bills or motions. The people of Ireland should be made owners of the land of Ireland but in no sense by confiscation. That briefly was the programme. The effort was blessed with great achievements. In a quiet determined, open manner the farmers combined to solve the many problems under which they were compelled to live.

In vain were representations made to the British Parliament, and the Land League then turned itself into a National Relief Organisation to meet the situation in the best manner they could.

The men who formed the Land League maintained it on the lines of its own open course and on the whole marvellously succeeded.

In the midst of these trials and distractions Fr. Cavanagh had the work of the parish to look after.

In those days the parish area comprised Knock and Aghamore and there were only two assistant priests — one at Knock and one at Aghamore.

It was to be expected that in view of the very disturbed times and in view of the hostility of an alien government towards everything Catholic and Irish, the youth would be in a backward state in religious instruction and even secular education.

The Archdeacon was now in Knock Parish thirteen years and signs of his great influence were beginning to show. Events in the area moved forward under the constant care and vigilance of the pastor.

All the hard-pressed essential needs were being provided gradually. Schools were built, teachers appointed, and all the usual chores calling for the attention of the pastor were dealt with.

Everything now appeared to be coming back to a state of normality.

The weather was about the only subject that was giving some uneasiness. There was a lot of rain falling. Sufficiently heavy and constant to arouse grave anxiety.

Potato blight was the great fear and at that time there was no knowledge of spraying with sulphate of copper to protect the crop.

The worst fears were, unhappily, realised, when the Autumn crop was about to be gathered and was found a complete failure. Now, there was nothing but a prospect of hunger and misery.

And, as if to comfort the people in a bitter hour of need, our Lady comes amongst them in visible form at the gable wall of the Parish Church.

Section II — The Apparition

It rained all day, the south-westerly wind carrying a thick mist against the gable wall of the parish church and in the quiet village of Knock there was not much astir.

The Beirnes' home was a neatly thatched cosy farmer's cottage about two hundred yards off the main road to the east of the church.

When evening came the wind and rain had abated nothing and, a little after seven o'clock, Margaret Beirne was sent to lock up the church for the night. Her work done and returning home she saw a sort of brightness over the church which she thought unusual but took no further notice. That Thursday evening, Mrs. Beirne and Mary, her daughter, had just returned from the health resort at Lecanvey, and visitors were in to welcome them back and to get all the news from the travellers.

There were lots of things to be talked about in those days — hard times, the famines, evictions, and, maybe, the Ladies' Land League.

Mary Beirne went out a piece of the road with the priest's housekeeper after her visit, and coming into view of the church gable, which was on the way remarked : "O, look at the statues. Why didn't you tell me the priest had got new statues for the chapel?" But Mary McLoughlin said she heard nothing about them and supposed the priest had left them outside the church. On coming nearer, however, Mary Beirne said : "But they're not statues, they're moving. It's the Blessed Virgin." She dashed back to the house to tell her mother and Dominic to come up to the chapel and see the lovely sight : "The Blessed Virgin was at the church gable."

Dominic, thinking Mary had gone strange, told her plainly not to be making a fool of herself. "Come up and see for yourself, then," she said, and at once returned to the chapel.

Her brother was alarmed and told the mother to follow Mary and take her home "before she makes a show of herself amongst the neighbours." But Dominic and the mother went up to the chapel and found that Mary was right.

And this is what the witnesses saw :

On the evening of the 21st of August, 1879, the vigil of the octave day of the Feast of Our Lady's Assumption, the parish church of Knock, Co. Mayo, was the scene of a singular and a beautiful spectacle.

At about half past seven that evening, and in daylight, an apparition of Our Blessed Lady, wearing a large brilliant crown and clothed in white garments was distinctly seen by some fifteen persons at the south gable wall of the church. Our Lady is described as having her hands raised as if in prayer and her eyes turned towards heaven. On her right hand was St. Joseph, his head inclined towards her, and on her left was St. John the Evangelist, attired as a bishop, his left hand holding a book and his right hand raised as if in preaching. To the left of St. John was an altar on which stood a cross and a Lamb, about 8 weeks old, around which the wings of angels hovered. The gable wall where this manifestation was seen was covered with a cloud of light, and the vision lasted for fully two hours.

During all the time rain fell heavily, yet the figures and the spot where they stood were quite dry.

The time at which the apparition appeared was some twenty minutes after sunset, so that by no law of radiation from reflected light could the images be thrown naturally or artificially from the clouds. Add to that the great fact that at the time the Blessed Virgin appeared it was pouring rain in torrents, which continued the whole time and late onwards through the night. The whole of that day had been one dreary, dismal downpour, from early dawn to the dusky hours of sundown.

Amongst the fifteen witnesses who were present at the Apparition was Mary McLoughlin, the housekeeper to Archdeacon Cavanagh.

On returning to the presbytery Mary McLoughlin told the Archdeacon of the wonderful vision of Our Blessed Lady at the gable wall of the church.

The Archdeacon himself refers to the fact of his absence from amongst the witnesses in the course of an interview with the correspondent of the "Weekly News," 14th February, 1880.

He said : "When my housekeeper returned home that night she said that she had seen the Blessed Virgin at the chapel. At first, I gave no serious attention to her words but afterwards when I began to think that a wonder may really have been witnessed, I concluded that the people did not leave the church until the Apparition was visible no longer.

"Ever since, this has been to me a cause of the deepest mortification. But I console myself with the reflection that it was the will of God that the Apparition should be shown to the people, not the priest.

"If I had seen it, and if I had been the first to speak of it, many things would have been said that cannot now be advanced with any fair shadow of reason or probability on their side."

The correspondent adds, ruefully :

"The strong emotion of the good pastor was so evident that both kept silent for some time."

Section III — Grave Crisis Averted
Secret Society Defied

The bad summer of 1879 led to another failure of the potato crop and our people were becoming alarmed that a repetition of 'Black '47" was at hand.

Young Ireland became restless and on the

move again. It was their duty to take whatever measures were necessary to lighten the imminent plight of the people.

Outside agitators were not wanting in the various districts in the West of Ireland and the usual secret meetings were organised. Here was discussed the land question in all its aspects and the district of Knock was selected as a place that required attention, particularly so because Fr. Cavanagh was preaching caution and restraint to his flock.

It was represented that the local parish priest was against the organisation and some means must be devised to deal with him, or whatever the corresponding phrase was used by our liberators in those days.

At a special secret meeting, therefore, the subject was fully discussed. Various suggestions were offered, but rejected. The extreme penalty was considered fitting to meet the menace of a dangerous priest who talked of the moral law, a man who warned his people about the danger of taking direction from unknown leaders, all on the same lines of those of "J.K.L.".

At length it was resolved that a lesser punishment than death would meet the position in the district. It would probably be sufficient warning to other parishes, especially when the "heads" had reached the conclusion that milder punishments were, at this stage, the correct procedure.

The proposal was made and carried, that the appropriate punishment for Archdeacon

Cavanagh was to have him subjected to a course of suitable threats and finally to have his ears cut off.

The local member was horrified at the whole turn of things, and made strenuous objections. He was overruled and reminded of his oath to the secret society and of the consequences to himself if he broke that oath.The penalty for such a breach was death.

The name of the man was decided and the day named for carrying out the impious proposition, to seize the Archdeacon and subject him to the mutilation decided by the heads of the organisation, whose names were unknown.

However, before the date fixed for the sacrilegious act the extraordinary events of the 21st August, 1879, had occurred at Knock. There was a complete change. The few who belonged to the vicinity of the parish and were aware of the dreadful decision now appeared to have received new courage. They denounced the whole proceedings.

They called together their friends in the parish and proclaimed they would rally round the pastor, regardless of consequences to themselves, and challenge any man to touch him.

The story of the Apparition had so impressed even the hardest of hearts that they regarded it as a direct sign through Our Lady that a crime of the kind contemplated was desecration of the basest sort and one that would assuredly cry to heaven.

There was no attempt to meet the challenge and the agitators remained away. There was no punishment meted out to the man who broke the secret society oath and defied the consequences. The spell was broken.

It was definitely a difficult position. Well meaning young men were faced with hungry families, pictures of Black '47 present to their minds. Hardships borne by their neighbours were calling out for redress and how could they remain inactive ?

We cannot refrain from paying tribute to those brave men of Knock and Aghamore who saved the parish from a crime, the strain of which could never be effaced.

They broke a terror and a tyranny that held our people in fear and dread for the best part of a century.

CHAPTER V

After The Apparition

IMMEDIATELY after the Apparition the Archdeacon's correspondence suddenly grew to eighty letters a day, entailing a truly formidable task for one already overwhelmed with countless other pressing tasks. He was indefatigable in his sacred and public duties and like another curé he went to bed at nine or sometimes ten. No one could be sure that he slept. There were people round the church. He made his way into the church, went down on his knees and asked God to bless the day that was beginning. He lit one or two tapers, sounded the Angelus bell himself, opened the door for pilgrims and took his seat in the confessional.

In order to gain time to deal with enquiries the Archdeacon addressed a letter to the Press for publication:

"Knock, Ballyhaunis,
February 12, 1880.

I will feel obliged if you will make it known to my numerous correspondents that it is simply impossible for me to answer the vast number of letters that arrive here daily from every part of Ireland, England and Scotland relative to the

Apparition of Our Blessed Immaculate Mother. I take this opportunity of stating that the reports given in the public journals are substantially correct, both as regards the Apparition and the numerous miracles wrought here since the 21st August last.

> I remain,
> Yours faithfully,
> Bartholomew Cavanagh, P.P."

There are many old letters from grateful invalids paying the highest tribute to the Archdeacon's remarkable kindness, courtesy and promptness in dealing with their requests. They express the warmest gratitude for the consolation and courage his beautiful letters always brought them in their trials and sufferings.

PILGRIMAGES BEGIN

The first organised Pilgrimage to Knock Shrine came from Limerick in March, 1880. It consisted of 50 members of the Holy Name Confraternity attached to the Redemptorist Church. There was no railway from Tuam to Claremorris in those days and it required nine open side-cars to convey the members from Tuam to the Shrine.

The Archdeacon's address on the occasion was reported in the "Munster News" of 24th March, 1880.

In the course of the sermon he said : . . .

God has always loved us, I may also say, in an especial manner; and now His own Mother Mary, the Queen of Heaven, has come down to visit us and comfort us in our trials.

She has not come alone. She brought with her St. Joseph, her beloved spouse and St. John, the beloved disciple, who rested on the bosom of Our Lord at the Last Supper.

St. John, who was given as a son to Our Blessed Lady, her pure spouse and her adopted son. She came to bless us, she, the Empress Queen of Heaven, accompanied by a retinue of Angels, who still remain with us, and whom we have seen with our own eyes. Not alone is there our own poor testimony to this, but the multitude of miracles wrought in and at the chapel prove it.

Mary loved Ireland as Ireland always loved Mary but she has not condescended visibly to visit our island as she has other lands. Now, she, the loving Queen of Heaven, has come down to us. She has come to us in our great grief and suffering to help us to be submissive to the will of God, and the blessings which she has brought are availed of by people from all parts. They come from England, France and Germany, from the United States and Canada, to seek Our Lady's help; and this little chapel in an obscure part of the world, is now known from the rising to the setting of the sun, and it seems destined by God to be the resort of pilgrims from all parts of the Catholic world . . .

After a formal presentation of the Pilgrimage

Banner, the Archdeacon, looking fondly at the banner, and evidently under deep emotion, burst forth into praise of Our Blessed Lady, thanked us for our act of public homage to the Blessed Virgin, and said blessings upon blessings would be returned to us. The good priest had his hands full of work, parochial duties and relief committees, with countless other calls upon his time, so we urged him to close the procession but he seemed very loath to leave, and we again formed our ranks and entered the chapel, singing a hymn to Our Lady.

Later in the same year there was a pilgrimage from the City of Cork and the people from there took occasion to make a presentation of the beautiful high altar which is at present in the church. It was erected by the Archdeacon in 1880. The altar is a replica of Foley's well-known work in Clarendon Street, Dublin. Both the altar and reredos were built by Scannel of Cork city. The style is Gothic. The materials composing the altar and tabernacle are Sicilian, Cork red, and Galway green marbles. The reredos is mainly Caen stone, relieved with panels of alabaster marble and jewels. It contains, besides figures of the Evangelists, two finely carved groups — one of the Nativity, the other Our Saviour at the final scene of the Temptation when angels came and ministered unto Him. A representation of the Agnus Dei is over the tabernacle and each of these is surrounded by a carved canopy rich in crocketting, finials, bosses and mouldings relieved by coloured marble spandrils and panels. The portion beyond the altar and on the same level is delicately diapered. The chief feature of the work however is the Pieta, a group, the members of which are nearly life-size, of the closing scene of the Passion. Its most prominent figure is that of Our Lord just taken down from the Cross, the body stretched at length, the chest raised somewhat from the ground by the right arm of our Blessed Lady on whose left hand rests the yielding arm of her Son, easy, as before the rigidity of death set in. St. John is represented kneeling at the head in the act of removing the Crown of Thorns.

Many impartial accounts were published of the impression made by the Archdeacon on those who visited Knock in the early days. Writing in 1882 to one of his Bishops a full account of his personal Pilgrimage to Our Lady's Shrine at Knock, the late Archbishop Lynch of Toronto, Canada, states as follows :

"The Ven. Archdeacon Cavanagh who had been hearing Confession came to salute us. He is a quiet, unassuming priest of middle age, tall and thin and ascetic looking and well calculated to make a favourable impression on all who approach him. This is another stroke of the providence of God to have such a priest in so celebrated a place that the pilgrims may carry away besides other gifts a great reverence for the priesthood of Ireland."

And he continues to describe the countryside as he found it :

"Alas, on the road from Claremorris to Knock I was saddened to death at seeing a number of cabins deserted, with the doors roughly walled up with cobble stones. Eighteen poor families were recently evicted from these miserable cabins and bad land. The scene of desolation was most oppressing and the more so when we considered the sufferings of the poor former inhabitants of these cabins. I visited a neat wooden cottage such as you would see in America, built on a safe piece of ground for a poor evicted family by the charity of the Ladies' Land League, without whose help thousands would have perished of cold and starvation. The children were some of the most graceful and beautiful I ever saw. They were evicted from the place of their birth and childish happiness. I thought that it was the most merciful condescension on the part of Our Immaculate Mother to appear in the neighbourhood of such a place and give the patience and courage of Saints and Martyrs to these poor people who had to bear a cross, one of the heaviest that could be imposed on a father, mother and children, to be driven from their homes by no fault of theirs but because in the mysterious ways of Providence, three bad harvests had deprived them of the means of paying their rents."

The "Daily Telegraph" Correspondent in one of his reports early in 1880 has the following :

"We drove to the cottage of the Parish Priest and found him in his garden whither he had gone perhaps for relaxation after getting through the multitude of letters that reach him by every post. Archdeacon Cavanagh is reputed along all the countryside as a man of simple piety, gentle manners, and a modest retiring disposition. This character is justified by his appearance. He at once makes a favourable impression and is about the last man in the world whom a stranger would look upon and suspect of anything but straightforward honest conduct. The V. Rev. gentleman gave his visitors a very cordial welcome and soon in the little parlour of his cottage I heard all that he could tell about the visions and miracles in which he believes with unquestioning and reverent faith."

There is another tribute recorded in the "Weekly News" of March, 1880 :

"Here is the abode of a devoted ecclesiastic whose reputation for sanctity has spread far beyond the sphere of his ministrations. The care of a large and mountainous parish makes exacting demands on the energies of body as well as mind and, hence it is little time Archdeacon Cavanagh has to spare from the calls of his spiritual stewardship, but of the time he can call his own, the greater part is spent before the altar of that church now linked with what may be perpetual fame."

One of the occasions, after the Apparition, that gave the Archdeacon great joy was to find a group from the Orphan-Magdalene home which he had founded in Westport more than twenty years previously, had made the long journey to Knock in a special party to visit the pastor of the Shrine and to petition. Our Lady's intercession in all their needs.

Apparition gable of Church in 1880, showing wall stripped of cement — taken by pilgrims and crutches left in thanksgiving for cures received.

The sanctuary of Church in 1880. The banner which Archdeacon Cavanagh received from the first organised pilgrimage (Holy Family Confraternity, Limerick, March 1880) can be seen on the right.

Knock Church in 1879 showing apparition gable on right and Archdeacon Cavanagh's cottage on left below.

Building erected by Archdeacon Cavanagh, as a retreat House, now St. Mary's Hostel. In a room on the second floor which is now a chapel - the Archdeacon died.

INTERIOR OF KNOCK CHAPEL

Interior of Knock Church showing altar presented by Cork City and erected by Archdeacon Cavanagh in 1880. The two oil paintings - left and right were the thanksgiving gifts for personal cures received by Archbishop Clune, Perth and Archbishop Murphy, Hobart.

Monstrance used by Archdeacon Cavanagh. It is now on view in Knock Museum.

Photograph of Archdeacon Cavanagh taken shortly after the apparition.

The Archdeacon as he was in later years.

The memorial tablet marking Archdeacon Cavanagh's grave. It is on the wall near Our Lady's altar in the apparition Church. See translation on Page118.

CHAPTER VI

Archdeacon's Diary of Cures

IT has been mentioned that claims of cures were being constantly made by pilgrims who visited Knock after the report of the Apparition.

It amazed everyone that the Archdeacon, although kept extremely busy with interviews and pilgrims' confessions, in addition to his own parish duties, yet found time to record accounts of these claims reported to him by pilgrims.

He did not make any entry until the Commissioners appointed by Archbishop McHale had concluded investigations and submitted their report.

Naturally, the period following the Apparition was marked by very deep devotion, penance and prayer. It was the time when there was a notable frequency in claims of cures, and so great was the impression borne on the ecclesiastical authorities, that a Commission of enquiry into the reported Apparition, and in conjunction with it, an investigation of the claims regarding cures, was set up within seven weeks of the Apparition.

The records left by Archdeacon Cavanagh in his Diary of Cures contain accounts of favours that could not be discounted, even without medical certificates to sustain them. We give a number of extracts from these, taken without any particular selection by way of special pleading. Amongst these will be found claims that were in their nature objective, organic, tangible, visible and sudden. The Medical Scientist approaches all claims of supernatural intervention with the greatest caution. He wants to have it quite clear that the complaint was of a kind like ulcers, fractures, malignant tumours, and not those that are purely emotional, nervous or based on auto-suggestion. To the scientific mind a miracle is an absurdity, and on principle it must proceed on lines to ensure that medical science will not be upset.

It would be difficult to disregard a claim like the case of the man from Cork, who had a polypus extending into the throat, and after the third day at Knock, coughed out the growth; or, the case of long standing cancer suddenly disappearing at the Shrine. Then, there is the verified record from Mr. Gibney of Dublin, now deceased, who asserted : "As the only person perhaps living who can recount with such intimate knowledge those extraordinary happenings, and I tremble, and fear lest I pass away without giving to future generations some knowledge, however meagre, however imperfect, of the mysterious occurrences that took place at Knock. I recall the scenes I witnessed, the sight of half a dozen stricken creatures undergoing simultaneously their cure or getting relief, and, in vision, I see the lame walk, my case included, the sightless seeing, the withered skin expanding."

We are also indebted to the late Miss M. Hartigan of Limerick County for her very vivid accounts of the pilgrims who in the old days on their way from the South of Ireland, called frequently at their country home for a night's rest. The memory of one such pilgrim remained clearly in her mind. It was the case of an elderly man who had a large, very unsightly growth on his neck, extending to his chest.

With the man was a young lad who assisted him on the way, as he was very weak due to the ailment. She and the other members of the family saw him setting out for Knock, leaning heavily on his stick, and a rosary beads in the other hand.

Some weeks later, the same pilgrim, on his return from Knock, called at the house again and spent the night there. She remembered the excitement of the household when they saw that the unsightly swelling had completely disappeared. He was cured while making a station at Knock.

Miss Hartigan's family were close friends of the Archdeacon. They always considered him an extremely spiritual man whose prayers were most powerful in seeking a favour from Our Blessed Lady. Her mother, who frequently visited the Shrine, told her of the great crowds that waited for the Archdeacon's blessing, and she knew people who suffered all their lives from agonising headaches to have been relieved at once after the blessing.

The great lesson that we learn from all these past records is the rigid penitential spirit that these suffering pilgrims and their friends, who visited the Shrine seeking favours, endured. It was the custom in those days for them to travel the hard road of penance under the most trying conditions. From the farthest point in Ireland the journey was made on foot for the most part. Strict fast was observed on the journey, most of it in silence and prayer, and always taking care to reach Knock in time to receive Holy Communion. There was no convenient transport by train or car for many years afterwards, and the time involved, together with the hard, selfimposed penance in those days, make modern pilgrimage with all its facilities seem very simple, casual affairs, indeed, and in some cases too suggestive of a day's outing or excursion.

We give many extracts from that portion of the Diary that has been preserved. As far back as 1880 upwards of 300 Cures were recorded.

Archdeacon Cavanagh's Diary is headed as follows :

Ad Majorem Dei Gloriam : 31st October, 1879

An account of the miraculous cures wrought at the gable of the chapel here where the Blessed Virgin Mary, the Immaculate Mother, appeared on the night of the 21st August, 1879. The cures have been wrought on persons who either prayed on the spot, or applied cement or clay, taken from the chapel, to the parts of the body affected by pains or wounds.

DEAFNESS AND VIOLENT PAIN IN EAR : On the 31st August, 1879 (ten days after the Apparition), a girl aged twelve years was cured while attending Mass at Knock. Her parents, Mr. and Mrs. P. J. Gordon of Claremorris, attested that Delia had suffered intensely all her life from deafness and violent pains in her left ear. Several times each week they had to get up in the night to try and relieve the awful pain by various remedies. She was stone deaf and for years used deaf and dumb alphabet. They took her on pilgrimage to Knock. While attending Mass there, the pain attacked Delia so badly that she began to cry and Mrs. Gordon had to bring her outside where they knelt in prayer before the place where the Apparition was seen. Mrs. Gordon picked out a piece of cement from the gable, made the sign of the Cross over it and placed it on the afflicted ear. Almost immediately the pain completely disappeared never to return and no trace of deafness remained. Her general health improved rapidly and in a very short time she became the picture of health and strength.*

* This was the first recorded cure in the Archdeacon's Diary. In 1946 Mr. Michael Gordon, brother of Miss Delia Gordon, confirmed in detail the account of his sister's cure. He added that she later went to U.S.A., and after a few years became head cashier in a furniture store known as "City of Paris" in Cincinnatti. Miss Gordon married a Mr. Shiers of Tulsa, Oklahoma, an engineer. In 1930 Delia died and from the day she was cured at Knock to her death she treasured the piece of cement taken from the gable wall of the church by her mother.

SERIOUS HAEMORRHAGE : Thomas Conlon of Shanvaghera. He was vomiting blood, was in a dying state, and received the last Sacraments of the Church which I administered to him. He was instantaneously cured by swallowing a few drops of water into which I had put a small piece of the cement taken from the Apparition gable. He has since been perfectly well.

SIGHTLESS EYE CAN SEE : Alice Dwyer, Kennaul, Co. Tipperary. Blindness of the right eye. She is twenty-nine years old and has been stone blind of the right eye all her life. The sight is now restored.

CANCER : Michael Corcoran from the Co. Meath. His cure has been quite complete as a result of his pilgrimage here.

FOOT USELESS FOR NINE YEARS : John O'Connor, of Ardagh, near Rathkeale. Has been for nine years unable to lay his left foot on the ground. He had to use an iron leg by the help of which he was able to move along very slowly. At Knock he received the use of the limb that had so long been useless, and went away rejoicing. The iron leg, which O'Connor left after him was placed in the receptacle for crutches and sticks at the church.

GROWTH EXTENDING INTO WINDPIPE : Jeremiah Sullivan, parish of Rathharry, Clonakilty, Co. Cork. Polypus, or flesh growth extending into the windpipe. He came to Knock with his father on Sunday, the 1st February, 1880, and got rid of his disease on the 4th. I saw the growth which he coughed up. The following is his statement : "I have been suffering from a hoarseness for the last eighteen months. I consulted four of the neighbouring doctors, one after the other, and to no avail, as none of them was able to ascertain the nature of the disease. Finding myself daily getting worse I came to the City of Cork, and consulted the most eminent doctor there. On the third day he found my ailment proceeded from a flesh growth or polypus in the windpipe. The conclusion the doctor came to was that there should be an operation, either externally or internally, either of which would be very dangerous. Hearing of the Apparition of the Blessed Virgin at Knock, I decided on visiting the place. I arrived on Sunday morning, February 1st. Thanks be to God and the Blessed Virgin Mary, I coughed off the polypus on the morning of the 4th February, after my third day's visit there."

SPINAL TROUBLE : Miss Bourke of Curraleigh (sister of Mr. W. Bourke, J.P., and of Surgeon Major Bourke) was cured in January, 1880. She was driven to Knock in her carriage in which she was placed lying, as if in bed. Four persons assisted in carrying her into the church. She prayed for some time before the altar, then to the delight and amazement of all, she got up and walked out of the church to her carriage. Some short time afterwards she came in thanksgiving and walked without difficulty. This lady had been an invalid for a long time.

SIGHT : Mrs. Curry's niece. She had been nearly blind. She could not see the steps at the entrance to the church. She visited Knock, and prayed there, and her sight has so far improved that she is able to distinguish objects even at a considerable distance.

VIOLENT RETCHING : There was a man living on Jones's Road, Dublin, of the name of Laurence Condron, who was very ill, and had a violent retching, and another disease also. A doctor was called in, but he could not stop it. The priest was also called in. I gave the invalid a little of the mortar from the Apparition gable and the moment he took it he got quite cured, and was here yesterday quite strong. There are plenty of witnesses of his being cured on the spot.

COMPLETE CURE OF DEAFNESS : A man from Barnacarroll was cured of deafness after he had been a victim to it for five years. The recovery of the sense of hearing was complete.

CONSTANT PAIN IN HEAD, ETC. : Brigid Curry, daughter of Mr. William Curry, of Lecarrow. Cured of constant pains in the head, and especially in the eyes and ears.

MENTAL TROUBLE : Mrs. Kilkenny of Woodfield, mental derangement and also a physical ailment that had defied the skill of the doctors.

ULCER ON FACE : Owen Mullarkey. Ulcer on the face. Cured after having lasted thirty years.

VIOLENT EPILEPSY : Patrick Kelly, Shammer,

Kilmovee. Epilepsy of a violent type. Cured by one visit.

LAMENESS : Ellen M'Loughlin, Killabeghagh. Lameness. She had suffered for three years past with her right foot. She could not touch the ground with it. A number of bones had been extracted from it at different times. She had to be carried on her way to Knock, but, while there, she recovered the full use of her foot, and walked on her return home.

EPILEPSY : A young man named Hopkins, second assistant in the National School, Claremorris, was cured of epilepsy.

CURE OF LEG : Mary Forestal, Caher, a girl of twelve. Was unable to make any use of one of her feet. Visited Knock, and returned home quite well.

CRIPPLED : Ellen Morris, Tarman, in the parish of Castlerea. Unable to walk at all for a period of two years. Completely cured at Knock on the 15th of January, 1880.

BLINDNESS : Mr. Conway, brother of Mrs. Curry. Cured of blindness. Bathed his eyes in water containing some of the cement. He was able to see on the following morning.

BLINDNESS : Honoria Cussane, parish of Kiltullagh. Cured by visiting Knock. It is stated on the authority of the Rev. P. M'Loughlin, parish priest of Kiltullagh (Co. Roscommon), that medical men had given up the case.

PALSY OF THE HEAD : Thomas Moran of Castles, parish of Kiltullagh (Co. Roscommon). Cured of palsy of the head.

BLINDNESS AND INTENSE PAINS : Anne O'Donnell, of the parish of Carracastle. Blindness and intense pains. She suffered such agony during a period of three years that her mother thought she would find her dead some morning. She is now restored to health and the use of sight.

PARALYSIS : Brigid Concannon, of the parish of Glan. Right foot powerless. Had been unable to move except by the help of two persons. By one visit to Knock was restored to the use of her limbs.

SIGHT : A man, whose name has not been ascertained received his sight in the church, before all the people while the Angelus bell was ringing on Thursday, the 29th of January, 1880.

EVIL : John Flynn, of Cloonmanagh, parish of Kilmovee. Cured of an evil. Medical remedies had all been tried in vain.

SIGHT RETURNS TO EYE AFTER 18 YEARS: Brigid Mary M'Nearey, Cloonfree, Co. Roscommon. Blindness of right eye. The eye had been sightless for the space of 18 years. The following letter affords the best evidence of this case that anyone could desire :

"Cloonfree,

Strokestown,

February 26, 1880.

Dear and Very Rev. Archdeacon,

It is with great pleasure I inform you that my eye still continues to improve. I had the great happiness of visiting Knock on the 2nd inst. On the following Wednesday, immediately after Mass I could see my hand for the first time this eighteen years, and every day since my sight is improving, thank God. In the year 1861 I received a severe wound in my right eye, the result of a piece of spring steel striking me by accident. All that could be done for me by medical skill was done, and of no avail. After a year's suffering I completely lost the sight, till the aforesaid date. I purpose, with God's help, to visit Knock on the 25th March next. Very Reverend Sir, no words could describe the happiness I feel in soul and body since I had the privilege of visiting that holy place. I beg to be excused for trespassing on your valuable time.

Thanking you for former kindness, believe me, very Rev. Sir,

Your faithful and obliged servant,

Brigid Mary M'Nerney."

HEART TROUBLE : Brigid Matilda Dillon. Weakness of the heart. The recovery in this case has been complete.

HIP DISEASE : Brigid Mary Galvin, Cork. Cured of hip disease. She had consulted several doctors, been five weeks in a Cork hospital, and seven months in one in Dublin, all to no good purpose.

RUNNING SORE OF 25 YEARS STANDING : John Nooran, parish of Clomnish, County Fermanagh. Cured of a running sore on the face. He had suffered from it for twenty-five years.

SIGHT RESTORED : A gentleman, caught cold in his right eye about twelve months ago. He suffered a great deal since, especially at night, and was obliged to give up writing. He placed himself under the care of two eminent medical men — one distinguished as an oculist — but no improvement was effected in the condition of his eye. By bathing it in water containing cement from Knock he has been cured.

PARALYSIS : Daniel M'Carty, Ryden, near Oldham, England. Paralysis. He had been unable to bring down his foot any lower than the level of the knee. Since his visit to Knock, he can stretch out the leg.

NOW ABLE TO STRETCH OUT LIMBS : Sarah Pierse, Meath Street, Dublin. Paralysis. For fourteen years she was unable to place either of her feet upon the ground. She had to be supported by a chair under each arm, and another, behind her back, and her legs were bent back beneath this latter. She suffered continually from pains the most intense. The pains are gone. She can now stretch out her limbs. And is improving in health and strength from day to day.

LAMENESS : John M'Mahon, Glasgow. Lameness. There were several evils in his leg and he had been unable to use it for two years, but on his visit to Knock experienced such an improvement that he left his crutch behind him.

NERVOUS TREMOR : John Mooney, parish of Drumlish. Cured of nervousness and constant tremor.

HEARING RETURNS AFTER TEN YEARS : Owen Halpin, Mell, Drogheda. Deafness. For ten years he had been quite deaf. On the 18th of February, the first day he ever visited Knock, he put a piece of the cement into his ear, and immediately recovered the power of hearing.

HIP DISEASE : John Brennan, parish of Curry, County Sligo. Hip disease. He has been suffering from the disease since Nov., 1878, and spent three months in hospital without any improvement in his condition. He is now almost as well as ever.

PAINS IN BACK, ETC. : Thomas Doherty. Cured of pains in the back and limbs, and general weakness. He had been twelve years subject to these ailments, and had consulted doctors without avail.

AFFLICTED JOINTS : John Finneran, Kilmovee. Pains and stiffness in the joints. He spent thirteen weeks in the infirmary of the Swinford workhouse. His ailments continued unimproved. He resolved to come to Knock. On his journey, he was not able any day to walk more than a quarter of a mile. Now he is able to walk as well as ever.

SORES ON HANDS AND FEET, ETC. : Thomas Cummins, of Strokestown. Sores on one of his hands and feet, and weakness of one arm. The sores have disappeared, and the arm, which used to be shockingly thin and all but entirely useless, has grown much fuller and stronger.

FIVE YEARS A CRIPPLE : Patrick Bourke, of Loughrea, County Galway. Paralysis. He had been five years a cripple, and had been a long time a patient in the Mater Misericordiae hospital, without any material bettering of his state. He left at Knock the crutch he had been so long obliged to use.

BENT FINGER, ETC. : Lucy Hegarty, of Meath. Pain in the left side, and stiffness of the little finger of the left hand. The finger, which had been bent in against the palm of the hand, is restored to its natural straightness, and the pain has been got rid of altogether.

PARALYSED FOR 20 YEARS : Margaret Nee,

of Moyrus. Paralysis. She had been in such an extreme degree deprived of the natural powers of motion that for twenty years she had been unable to go from one place to another except upon her hands and knees. Since her visit to Knock, her right leg has straightened. She is able to stretch it out and move it freely. The left leg is beginning to extend and become flexible.

INSOMNIA : An exalted dignitary of the Church, who had been suffering from sleeplessness for several weeks together, was cured by having placed under his pillow a piece of the cement from Knock. The night succeeding he slept profoundly, and has not since been troubled by want of sleep.

EPILEPSY : Michael Martin of Lissaculleen, Co. Monaghan. Cured of epilepsy.

TEN YEARS A CRIPPLE : Mary Ryan, of Thurles. Had been for ten years unable to go on her knees, or to move one inch without the help of a crutch. Her recovery enabled her to leave her crutch at Knock.

BLINDNESS : Mary O'Dea, parish of Kilmacduagh. Cured of blindness of the right eye.

HEART TROUBLE : Pat Flanagan, Cloontuskert. Cured of a heart affection.

VIOLENT PAINS IN HEAD : A daughter of Mr. Mark O'Brien, of Cloonahulty, was suffering so intensely from violent pains in the head that for days together her parents thought her life in imminent danger. She drank some water containing a portion of the cement, fell asleep, and woke quite well.

TWENTY-TWO YEARS DEAF : On the same day the writer, and the witnesses with him, saw at Knock chapel a woman, aged about twenty-eight, who had been deaf since she was six years old, receive the power of hearing. The writer spoke to her, and she heard as well as anyone gifted with the faculty of hearing.

PARALYSIS : Sarah Morrisroe, of Woods, parish of Ballaghy. Paralysis. Mr. Ignatius O'Donel of Swinford, bears testimony to her case in the following terms : "I saw her myself on or about the 22nd December, when she had not the use of her limbs, and on seeing her yesterday, after she had walked seven miles, she did not seem to be a bit tired." — Ignatius O'Donel, Swinford, February 5th, 1880.

SIGHT RETURNS : Thomas McNamara, of the County Tipperary, recovered his sight, both eyes were dim, and he was obliged to have a guide with him coming to Knock.

INCURABLE MALADY : Mrs. Nedham of St. Andrew's parish, Glasgow, was the victim of some terrible malady, incurable by the aid of human agency, is fully restored to her former good health.

CATARACT DISAPPEARS : John Carroll of Tipperary, was suffering form a cataract on his left eye. Is perfectly cured of same.

HEARING RESTORED : Martin Loughran of the parish of Milltown, County Kildare, who was deaf since he was three years of age, got his hearing here to-day. He was attended formerly by Drs. Wilde and Wilson, without any good results for him.

PAINS AND ROLLING OF EYES : Anne Fox, of the County Meath, is cured of the constant involuntary rolling of the eyes and pains in the head.

SPINAL AND HIP DISEASE : Kate Kennedy, County Tipperary, parish of Gurtnaho, was suffering for two years and a half from spinal and hip disease, and was in one of the hospitals in Dublin and left it uncured. She is now quite well and fully recovered.

SEVERE PAINS : Widow John Kelly of Morpeth, County of Northumberland (Rev. M. Davey is P.P.), was suffering severe pains in her back and legs, and could not work or even sometimes turn in her bed during the past five years. Has been completely cured the second time she went on her knees in the chapel here.

BAD MENTAL TROUBLE : Patrick Cross, of the City of Limerick, is cured of insanity, from which he was suffering for the last four months. He was for six weeks in the lunatic asylum of Limerick. He was brought out incurable, and against the will of the doctor. he is as sound now in mind and body as any man in Ireland. He was also suffering from a weakness in the back, and could not walk without a stick, and he can now walk home without it. He is perfectly cured.

HEART TROUBLE & GENERAL DEBILITY : Mathew Clarke, County Tipperary, is cured of stiffness in both legs and weakness of his limbs and general debility, due to heart trouble. He could not walk a quarter of a mile without being in danger of falling.

DEAFNESS AND PAIN FOR 20 YEARS : Martin O'Donnel, Ballycastle, Mayo, is cured of deafness in the left ear from which he suffered twenty years accompanied with great pain. He is now quite well and cured of both.

STONE BLIND FOR 4 YEARS : Mary Nolan, of Kildare, who has for years been stone blind, got her sight.

PALPITATION : Joseph Fagan, of Moyvore, Westmeath, was cured of palpitation of the heart and general debility. He was under the care of doctors both at home and in America, and to no purpose. He is cured now.

BORN WITH TURNED FOOT : Cornelius Driscoll, of Cardiff, South Wales, was born with a turned foot and wore an iron strap on his right foot since he was twelve months old. He is now fourteen years of age and he is perfectly cured, and he can walk, as he did to-day, two miles without the strait iron shoe.

DEAF AND DUMB FROM BIRTH : Miss Katie Reilly who worked as a cook and known to Mrs.

Bennett, of 62 Sunday's Well, Cork, was born deaf and dumb. In the early days of Knock Shrine she visited it as a pilgrim seeking cure, being then over 21 years old. One evening during Benediction of the Blessed Sacrament the dumb girl recovered her speech fully and she never lost it again.

CHAPTER VII

Death of Archdeacon Cavanagh

THE Archdeacon had been in failing health for a few years before the end of his life. He was still living in his own little three-roomed thatched cottage already mentioned, for which he had a very special affection. Those who knew him intimately said his deep attachment to so poor a dwelling was due to the many favours he had received there from Our Blessed Lady. It was only towards the end that he reluctantly agreed to be removed to the building nearby which he had erected, and which he had intended as a retreat house for men run by a body of priests. Afterwards, this building was for a time used as a Parochial house, and later — about 1930 — it passed to the Sisters of Charity of St. Vincent de Paul who have since conducted it as a Hostel for pilgrims, and is now known as St. Mary's Hostel. The room used as the Oratory for the Community and where Holy Mass is celebrated, is the room which Archdeacon Cavanagh occupied during the period of his last illness, and in which he died.

In his final illness the Archdeacon was attended and fortified by the rites of Holy Church by the late Canon Reidy, who was then a young Curate in Claremorris. It was the Archdeacon's wish that Father Reidy would be with him at the end. Canon Reidy recalled how the local priests marvelled that the Archdeacon lingered on for days, as they all expected his death every moment. Father Reidy felt that it seemed the Archdeacon was waiting to die on the great Feast of the 8th December, and around about the hour of midnight on that date, his spirit departed. Then the people, as soon as possible filed in, anxious to touch the body with rosaries and other devotional objects and to obtain some little memorial of their devoted pastor, whom they loved and looked upon as a most saintly sagart.

It was then the parish and in fact the whole country resounded with praise and stories of the virtues of the dead pastor, and they had no hesitation in calling him a singularly holy priest. They related the commonly accepted pious belief that the Apparition at Knock could be entirely attributed to the holiness of their pastor. They told of his penances, his self-denials, and they talked in no uncertain manner of the hair shirt which he had worn the greater part of his life. In the course of a severe illness the Archdeacon's sister removed the shirt and for a long time it remained at Caltra, Co. Galway, in the home of his nephew . . . And, indeed, it was freely accepted in the parish that the Archdeacon was frequently favoured with visits of Our Lady in his own little cottage. Once when questioned by a friend on this point, the Archdeacon replied that there were a great many other manifestations of which he would not care to speak. And some of the stirring events that occurred after the Apparition were recalled by the people; also, to tell of the many occasions when young men, on the run, hastened to the Archdeacon late at night seeking Confession, and the Sacraments. Those young men on their way, afoot, via Cobh to America frequently took in Knock on the route, asking Our Lady's blessing and protection on a hazardous journey.

Writing home some time ago one of them related how, one night, he with others called at the Archdeacon's house. It was necessary to travel by dark because they were marked down for arrest under the Coercion Acts dealing with the Land agitation. They knocked at the house and, although there was no one residing there, except the Archdeacon, the door was opened by a stranger who appeared to know of their mission without any explanation.

They were told the priest had a strenuous day and was resting for the night, and were asked to return early next morning when he would hear their confessions and give them Holy Communion. Next morning they had an interview with Archdeacon Cavanagh and told him of their experience in his cottage; of the peace and holy joy that filled them while the stranger was speaking and giving them directions as regards their journey, etc. The Archdeacon asked them not to speak of this until after his death and they had faithfully kept that promise.

It was freely believed that the stranger was some heavenly visitor, an event that the people accepted as quite a common happening at the Archdeacon's house.

One of his past curates (the late Monsignor McAlpine) put on record a remarkable tribute to the pastor's holiness and priestly qualities. In the course of an account written to "The Lamp," then the most important Catholic paper in the world, he wrote as follows :

"On the Feast of the Immaculate Conception last year (1897) there passed away one of the most remarkable and, in a sense, the most conspicuous figure among Irish ecclesiastics. A man of extraordinary piety, self-sacrifice, zeal and generosity. The Venerable Archdeacon Cavanagh has been mourned by the thousands who knew and esteemed him. He passed from the scene of many strange events on the day when, perhaps, he was desirous that all that was mortal of him should cease to live, and yielding up the ghost must have been to him a singularly easy transition from one sphere to another, for he had lived a life of wonderful austerity and devotion.

"The pastor of Our Lady's Shrine at Knock was noted for one peculiar system of devotion — that of the Immaculate Mother — and for that devotion he lived and worked and made his mission here one ceaseless effort at diffusing the glories of Mary and the eternal wisdom of her Son.

"He had that strange and rare temperament sometimes to be found among the old school of Irish priests, in which all that was intensely spiritual was developed to a high degree, frequently distinguishing his character for all that is genuinely pious above the heads of his brethren. To take him away from the piety to which he had devoted his whole life would have been to separate one ingredient from another to the total destruction of both. One element was profound absorbing spirituality, the other a consuming, overwhelming charity to all men, a boundless system of generosity, strange, peculiar and even weird in its extraordinary method.

"We can only judge of a man by his actions and by his most essential characteristics and those of the Archdeacon were the powerful antithesis of all that is unspiritual and ungenerous. But it is needless to dwell upon a point in a character which to those who knew him was the most conspicuous and apparently the most unstudied.

"To write a resume of such a life would require nothing but the record of years of devotion to the one common purpose for which he aimed, struggled, fought, and finally won.

"The lamented Archdeacon passed away at Knock where, since 1867, he spent his life.

"It has been said that he had no banking account which was true enough for he never had anything to put into one. All that he ever had went to the poor and although he was often well supplied with money from various sources he spread it amongst his poor with a free hand and a beneficent disposal discreet but generous. He was in many ways like a Cure d'Ars and like him he was spontaneous in his actions of goodness, prayer and almsgiving. He was indeed an ideal priest, a man of great force of character and spiritual superiority."

The vast concourse, clergy and laity, that attended the obsequies to mourn and pray for the repose of the soul of a grand priest, spoke of the honour and respect in which he was held by all.

Amongst the clergy were the late Dr. McEvilly, Archbishop of Tuam, priests from the surrounding districts, and members of religious orders.

The laity were present in large numbers to pay a last tribute of respect to a deceased priest who was known to them for a long time as the kindly, charitable, courteous pastor of Our Lady's Shrine at Knock.

His mortal remains were laid to rest within the church on the epistle side facing Our Lady's altar and opposite the marble inscription on the West wall, near the 13th Station of the Cross.

The memorial tablet erected to the memory of the Archdeacon is itself a very remarkable tribute from his parishioners :

ORATE PRO ANIMA
VENERABILIS BARTHOLOMEW
CAVANAGH
ARCHDIACONI CAPITULI TUAMENSIS
ET
PAROCHI DE KNOCK ET AGHAMORE
CUJUS FAMA OB EXIMIAM EJUS VITAE
SANCTITATEM ET DEIPARAE DEVOTIONEM
LONGE   LATEQUE   DIFFUSA   EST.
INDEFFESUS IN TRIBUNALI ASSIDUUS IN
LABORIBUS PIIS PLENUS ANNIS ET
MERITIS MORTUUS EST DIE 9a (recte 8)
DECEMBRIS A.D. 1897
R.I.P.

PAROECIA GRATA PASTORI
VENERATO HOC MEMORIALE ERIXIT.

TRANSLATION

Pray for the Soul of the Venerable Batholomew Cavanagh, Archdeacon of the Chapter of Tuam, and Parish of Knock-Aghamore, whose fame, on account of the extraordinary sanctity of his life, and his devotion to the Mother of God, was diffused far and wide. Unwearying in the confessional, assiduous in works of piety, he died, full of years and merits, December 9 (recte 8), 1897, R.I.P.

A grateful parish erected this memorial to a venerated pastor.

The inscription is an unusually close summary of the whole priestly life of the Archdeacon. True, indeed, were the fame of his sanctity and his outstanding devotion to Mary known far and wide, and his assiduity in all pious works, especially his untiring efforts in the Confessional.

For thirty years this devoted pastor preached the Blessed Virgin — the ever Immaculate Mother of God — at Knock and what was more a fitting close to such a life than that he should be called to his eternal reward about the midnight hours of the 8th December, 1897, the Feast of the Immaculate Conception of Our Blessed Lady.

One may hope and pray that the memory of

The Basilica of Our Lady of Knock, Queen of Ireland.
Blessed and dedicated by Cardinal William Conway of Armagh - 18-7-1976.

Pope John Paul II in prayer within the Shrine "the goal of my journey to Ireland" the Apparition in every detail.

ter which he blessed the magnificent white marble statuary which represents

Having blessed the statues the Pope is led by Archbishop Joseph Cunnane to light the Family Life Candle : 30-9-1979.

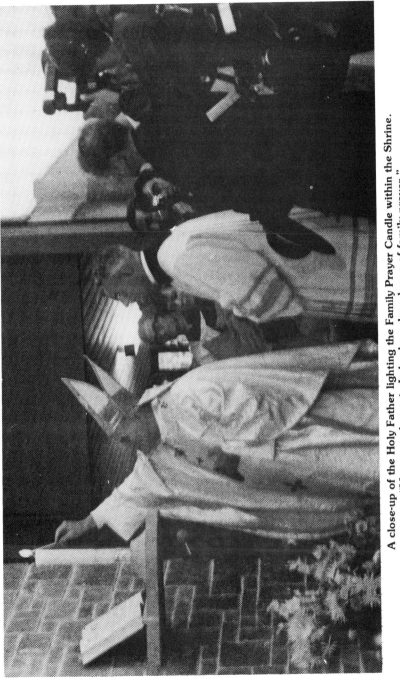

A close-up of the Holy Father lighting the Family Prayer Candle within the Shrine.
"May every home in Ireland . . . be a home of family prayer."

Adoration Chapel which was blessed by Most Rev. Dr. Joseph Cunnane, Archbishop of Tuam, on the Feast of Corpus Christi - 2-6-1983.

The New Chapel of Reconciliation was blessed by Most Rev. Dr. Joseph Cassidy, Archbishop of Tuam on 15-7-1990.

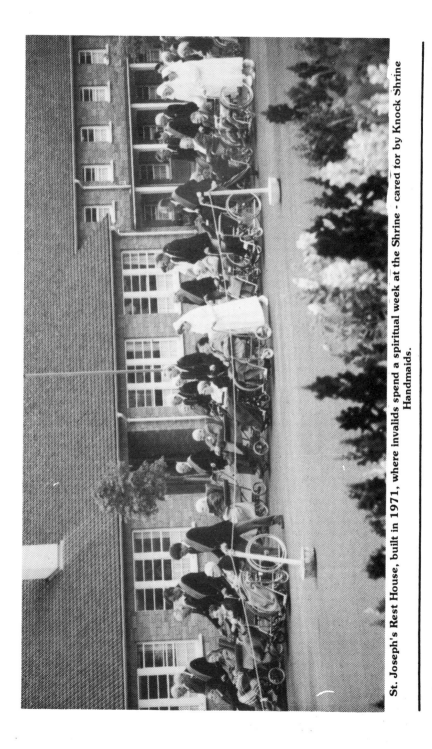

St. Joseph's Rest House, built in 1971, where invalids spend a spiritual week at the Shrine - cared for by Knock Shrine Handmaids.

A view of the New Shrine from the East with the Papal Cross on the right and pilgrims present on the occasion of the pilgrimage of Mother Teresa of Calcutta - 5th June, 1993.

Front view of New Shrine enclosing Apparition Gable, which was blessed by Most Rev. Dr. Joseph Cassidy, Archbishop of Tuam - 10-5-1992.

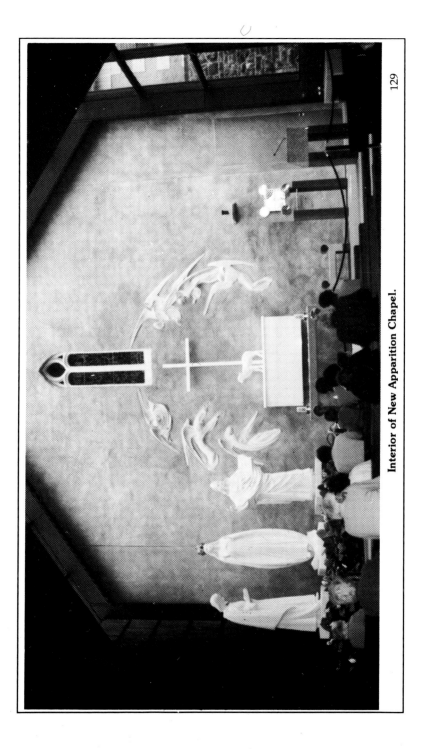

Interior of New Apparition Chapel.

Knock Shrine Museum built in 1987. A large section is reserved for information relating to Archdeacon Cavanagh.

Archdeacon Cavanagh who has been described as a man of "profound, absorbing spirituality," "of consuming over whelming charity," "with a boundless system of generosity and extraordinary self-sacrifice," will influence his people and the many pilgrims who come to the Shrine of Our Lady of Knock.

May his memory help us also in a continuance of the spirit of those early penitential days which were so marked by favours, spiritual and temporal. For nothing would be more displeasing than a departure from the proper spontaneous single purpose spirit of devotion and penance that the pilgrims rigidly observed in those days.

It would certainly be pleasing to the Archdeacon to see the multitudes at the present day, who come on pilgrimage to Knock Shrine, prepared to assist at Mass, receive Holy Communion and take part in the devotions to which he was so attached, the Stations of the Cross and the recitation of the Rosary.

What a joy it would be to one who loved "The Ever Immaculate Mother of God" so intensely, to see her publicly honoured and her statue borne shoulder high by young men from all over Ireland and even beyond the seas, each Sunday in procession.

A HOPE FOR THE FUTURE

"We cherish the hope that Mary will continue to manifest more and more, her great power at this shrine, and that she will give a gracious answer to the prayers of her children who come here to honour her and to seek her intercession.

"It was by prayer that Knock has become what it is to-day. It is by prayer that, please God, Knock will become still greater in the years to come. We piously believe that the Blessed Mother of God sanctified this ground by her visible presence over seventy years ago. And we believe that she continues to bless it by a presence, which, though no longer visible is not less powerful or merciful. We believe that it is her wish that her children come here on pilgrimages and pray in procession and in private, and that she will show a Mother's tender love, and manifest her Mother's power. And for this belief, we have the testimony of credible witnesses. But we have another mighty foundation for our faith, the unshaken confidence of the Irish people in this Shrine of Knock. For nearly three-quarters of a century, through fair weather and through foul, they have come in their thousands and have made a path to this humble church. Every inch of this chapel yard has been sanctified by the footprints of men and women who are high in heaven to-day. And many of them are there because of the sacrifices they made to honour Mary, and because of the graces they received within the hallowed walls of this shrine. You may be sure that long line of Ireland's hidden saints, who tramped the roads of Ireland to Knock, wet and weary and hungry and footsore, in those dark days of our country, are looking down on you in the Beatific Vision. You can count on them to help you. But they in turn, look to you, to hold high the torch which Mary kindled on this hill, and which they took from her blessed hands, and kept burning down the years, and have handed on to you. We must keep faith with those great souls, the pilgrims of the past. Pray then. Pray the Rosary especially, that the true pilgrim spirit may abide here, in our day and in the generations to come. Mary will bless Knock in proportion as we try to be worthy of her blessing. Pray that each pilgrim who comes, may experience Mary's presence and Mary's power, and may leave with that peace and joy of heart which Mary always obtains for her clients.

"Here you have a shrine that has been built not with material stones, but with gems far more precious, the millions of rosaries that loving hearts and worn fingers have laid all these years at the feet of Our Lady of Knock."*

* Rev. Paul Waldron speaking at Knock Shrine, April, 1950.

Epilogue

ONE can hardly avoid dwelling on the strong parallel in the lives of the Cure d'Ars and our Archdeacon Cavanagh. Both were parish priests; both lived in the greater part of the nineteenth century; both were favoured reputedly by visions of our Blessed Lady; they were both confronted with the evils of secret societies; both knew the rigours and effects of persecution; and there were two very important features common to the pastors — their abiding courtesy to all and their indefatigable efforts in the confessional.

M. Gheon tells us when M. Vianney (Cure d'Ars) learned that in the long roll of the ages not a single parish priest had been raised to the Church's altars as a saint. Popes had been canonised, cardinals and bishops, religious and laymen; but of parish priests not one, not the shadow of one. The melancholy inference was there was no condition in the whole world in which sanctity was more difficult to attain. That was why the Cure was so unsure of himself.

The canonised enjoy the official seal of the Church and are entitled to be called "Saint" but no one would venture to suggest that there are no uncanonised saints amongst the parish priests. Their names must be legion. So M.

Vianney has himself broken the spell of official silence for, in 1905 he was declared Venerable by Pope Pius X and Patron of all the priests having charge of souls in France, and in 1924 the process of the Cure d'Ars was brought to its final stage when Venerable M. Vianney was formally raised to the altar by Pope Pius XI under the title, Saint John Marie Baptiste Vianney.

Saint John Baptiste is now a great patron and advocate of all the parish priests, for he knows their responsibilities; their lonely lives; their anxious care of the souls entrusted to them; having a vigilant eye for the erring members of the flock; and suffering with their people in their trials and rejoicing with them in their triumphs.

May be, one day, in God's own time and plan, we, too, shall rejoice to see the cause of Archdeacon Cavanagh introduced for the official examination of Holy Church.